EARTHQUAKES

Plate Tectonics and Earthquake Hazards

THE HAZARDOUS EARTH

EARTHQUAKES

Plate Tectonics and Earthquake Hazards

Timothy Kusky, Ph.D.

Facts On File
An imprint of Infobase Publishing

EARTHQUAKES: Plate Tectonics and Earthquake Hazards

Facts On File, Inc.
An imprint of Infobase Publishing
132 West 31st Street
New York NY 10001

Library of Congress Cataloging-in-Publication Data
Kusky, Timothy M.
Earthquakes: plate tectonics and earthquake hazards / Timothy Kusky.
p. cm.—(Hazardous Earth)
Includes bibliographical references and index.
ISBN-13: 978-0-8160-6462-5 (acid-free paper)
ISBN-10: 0-8160-6462-8 (acid-free paper)
1. Earthquakes. 2. Plate tectonics. I. Title.
QE534.3.K87 2008
551.22—dc22   2007020832

Facts On File books are available at special discounts when purchased in bulk quantities for businesses, associations, institutions, or sales promotions. Please call our Special Sales Department in New York at (212) 967-8800 or (800) 322-8755.

You can find Facts On File on the World Wide Web at http://www.factsonfile.com

Text design by Erika K. Arroyo
Illustrations by Richard Garratt

Printed in the United States of America

VB FOF 10 9 8 7 6 5 4 3 2 1

This book is printed on acid-free paper and contains 30 percent post-consumer recycled content.

*To the Himalayan villagers whose lives were changed
by the Kashmir earthquake of October 8, 2005*

■ ■ ■

Contents

Preface

Natural geologic hazards arise from the interaction between humans and the Earth's natural processes. Recent natural disasters such as the 2004 Indian Ocean tsunami that killed more than a quarter million people and earthquakes in Iran, Turkey, and Japan have shown how the motion of the Earth's tectonic plates can suddenly make apparently safe environments dangerous or even deadly. The slow sinking of the land surface along many seashores has made many of the world's coastal regions prone to damage by ocean storms, as shown disastrously by Hurricane Katrina in 2005. Other natural Earth hazards arise gradually, such as the migration of poisonous radon gas into people's homes. Knowledge of the Earth's natural hazards can lead one to live a safer life, providing guidance on where to build homes, where to travel, and what to do during natural hazard emergencies.

The eight-volume The Hazardous Earth set is intended to provide middle- and high-school students and college students with a readable yet comprehensive account of natural geologic hazards—the geologic processes that create conditions hazardous to humans—and what can be done to minimize their effects. Titles in the set present clear descriptions of plate tectonics and associated hazards, including earthquakes, volcanic eruptions, landslides, and soil and mineral hazards, as well as hazards resulting from the interaction of the ocean, atmosphere, and land, such as tsunamis, hurricanes, floods, and drought. After providing the reader with an in-depth knowledge of naturally hazardous processes, each volume gives vivid accounts of historic disasters and events that have shaped human history and serve as reminders for future generations.

One volume covers the basic principles of plate tectonics and earthquake hazards, and another volume covers hazards associated with volcanoes. A third volume is about tsunamis and related wave phenomena, and another volume covers landslides, soil, and mineral hazards, and includes discussions of mass wasting processes, soils, and the dangers of the natural concentration of hazardous elements such as radon. A fifth volume covers hazards resulting from climate change and drought, and how they affect human populations. That volume also discusses glacial environments and landforms, shifting climates, and desertification—all related to the planet's oscillations from ice ages to hothouses. Greater understanding is achieved by discussing environments on Earth that resemble icehouse (glaciers) and hothouse (desert) conditions. A sixth volume, entitled *The Coast*, includes discussion of hazards associated with hurricanes, coastal subsidence, and the impact of building along coastlines. A seventh volume, *Floods*, discusses river flooding and flood disasters, as well as many of the contemporary issues associated with the world's diminishing freshwater supply in the face of a growing population. This book also includes a chapter on sinkholes and phenomena related to water overuse. An eighth volume, *Asteroids and Meteorites*, presents information on impacts that have affected the Earth, their effects, and the chances that another impact may occur soon on Earth.

The Hazardous Earth set is intended overall to be a reference book set for middle school, high school, and undergraduate college students, teachers and professors, scientists, librarians, journalists, and anyone who may be looking for information about Earth processes that may be hazardous to humans. The set is well illustrated with photographs and other illustrations, including line art, graphs, and tables. Each volume stands alone and can also be used in sequence with other volumes of the set in a natural hazards or disasters curriculum.

Acknowledgments

Many people have helped me with different aspects of preparing this volume. I would especially like to thank Carolyn, my wife, and my children, Shoshana and Daniel, for their patience during the long hours spent at my desk preparing this book. Without their understanding, this work would not have been possible. Frank Darmstadt, executive editor, reviewed and edited all text and figures, providing guidance and consistency throughout. Many sections of the work draw from my own experiences doing scientific research in different parts of the world, and it is not possible to thank the hundreds of colleagues whose collaborations and work I have related in this book: Their contributions to the science that allowed the writing of this volume are greatly appreciated. I have tried to reference the most relevant works, or, in some cases, more recent sources that have more extensive reference lists. Any omissions are unintentional.

Introduction

Every day parts of the surface of the Earth are rattled by earthquake tremors and, occasionally, some regions are shaken violently during earthquakes, resulting in widespread damage and destruction. This book discusses the processes and causes of earthquakes and strives to give readers an understanding of why they occur, where they are most likely to happen, and what the effects of major earthquakes are likely to be.

The Earth is a dynamic planet composed of different internal layers that are in constant motion, driven by a vast heat engine deep in the planet's interior. The cool surface layer is broken into dozens of rigid tectonic plates that move around on the surface at rates of up to a few inches (cm) per year, driven by forces from the internal heat and motion in the partly molten layers within the planet. Most destructive earthquakes are associated with motions of continents and ocean floor rocks that are part of these rigid tectonic plates riding on moving parts of the Earth's interior. Plate tectonics is a model that describes the process related to the slow motions of more than a dozen of these rigid plates of solid rock around on the surface of the Earth. The plates ride on a deeper layer of partially molten material that is found at depths starting at 60–200 miles (100–320 km) beneath the surface of the continents, and 1–100 miles (1–160 km) beneath the oceans. The motions of these plates involves grinding, sticking, and sliding where the different plates are in contact and moving in different directions, causing earthquakes when sudden sliding motions occur along faults. These earthquakes release tremendous amounts of energy, raising mountains and, unfortunately, sometimes causing enormous destruction.

Earthquakes: Plate Tectonics and Earthquake Hazards presents the main ideas of plate tectonics, and will give readers an understanding of how, why, and where most earthquakes occur. The book also describes what happens during earthquakes, using many examples of hazards such as landslides, passage of seismic-earthquake waves through the ground, and other phenomena that people have encountered during real earthquakes. The furious power of nature is unleashed during earthquakes and, by reading this volume, the reader will gain an appreciation of the relentless forces that constantly build up within the Earth. Finally, the book presents descriptions of events that might be experienced by someone in the unfortunate circumstance of being in a real and severe earthquake. This knowledge is mixed with advice that might be used to make friends and family safer during an earthquake and its aftermath, potentially saving lives.

Part one of this book consists of four chapters that describe the main components of the theory of plate tectonics and uses many examples to illustrate each main process. The first chapter introduces readers to the planetary-scale arrangement of different layers in the Earth and about the varied landforms found on the surface. The Earth has deep oceans, high mountains, and vast plains that have elevations close to sea level. It turns out that plate tectonics can explain why the major landforms of the surface of the planet have such distinctive forms. This introductory chapter includes a concise but fairly detailed description of how plate tectonics works, including a discussion on the forces inside the planet, and it includes discussion of the different types of processes and events that occur along the three main types of boundaries among the plates. The second through fourth chapters examine details and real examples of where and how plates move apart, toward each other, or slide past each other along plate boundaries. At divergent boundaries, new crust is formed in the space that opens between plates that are being torn apart by forces from deep inside the planet. At convergent boundaries, plates are moving toward each other and one plate either sinks back into the interior of the Earth or large mountains are formed where they collide. The third main type of boundary, a transform margin, forms where the plates simply slide past each other, as along California's San Andreas Fault. The most destructive earthquakes are associated with the convergent and transform margins, whereas divergent boundaries usually have small to moderate-sized earthquakes. Each type of plate boundary is discussed separately, and illustrated with a focused discussion in a sidebar about one area in the world that best illustrates that type of boundary.

Part two of the book consists of four chapters that focus on earthquakes and how they form, and what effects they have on humans and society. The first chapter of this section (the fifth chapter of the book) discusses the origins of earthquakes and how geologists and seismologists measure them. The Richter scale is the most commonly used method to portray the amount of energy released in a quake although other methods may be better in some situations. Each increase of one (such as 5.0 to 6.0) on the Richter scale corresponds to a more than ten times increase in the amount of energy released during an earthquake. Therefore a magnitude 8 earthquake releases much more than 100 times as much energy as a magnitude 6 earthquake. In the sixth chapter, the many types of hazards associated with earthquakes are discussed and illustrated with many real and devastating examples. These hazards include the sudden movement of the ground, passage of different types of seismic waves, landslides, liquefaction where the ground suddenly starts to behave like a fluid, in addition to other phenomena like tsunamis and fires. Major earthquakes may be associated with many of these hazards, making them truly horrific events. In the seventh chapter, several different and experimental methods of trying to predict earthquakes are discussed, and presented in terms of how much advance warning these systems may give to people in affected areas. Earthquake prediction and warning is not yet an exact science and much research needs to be done to help give people a greater warning about when earthquakes might strike.

Chapter eight consists of a series of accounts of some of the most significant and disastrous earthquakes to have affected the human race throughout history. Descriptions of these events include discussion of the plate tectonics setting of the earthquake, the hazards that became disasters, and how these natural processes affected people of the region. Millions of people have died during earthquakes, and many of these could have been saved if they had lived in safer, stronger buildings, or if others were able to react fast enough to help devastated regions. We hope that this book will help save lives in the future.

Part I

■ ■ ■

Plate Tectonics

1

General Earth Structure
and Plate Tectonics

U nderstanding earthquake hazards begins with an understanding of how the planet Earth formed and how its internal heat engine drives tectonic plates to move around on the surface. This chapter reviews the formation of the Earth and then discusses the main divisions of the Earth's interior in terms of physical and chemical layers. Heat loss from the deep interior drives the plate tectonic engine, forcing large rigid plates to move around on the surface, grinding past each other, forming earthquakes. Surface landforms reflect the type of plate boundary or interior the region represents, so descriptions of the characteristics of major landforms associated with different tectonic plate boundaries are included in this chapter. Finally, a discussion of how plate tectonics works includes detailed descriptions of geological processes at the three main types of plate boundaries, including examples of each process.

The Earth is one of a group of eight planets that condensed from a solar nebula in the Milky Way galaxy about 5 billion years ago (until recently, the solar system was thought to contain nine planets, but in 2006 a group of astronomers voted that Pluto did not meet the criteria to be a true planet, so its status as a planet was revoked). The process of condensation began with a great swirling cloud of hot dust, gas, and proto-planets that collided with each other, sticking together with each collision, eventually forming the main planets. The growth or accretion of the Earth from these smaller bodies was a high-temperature process that caused the melting of the early planet Earth, forming what scientists call a magma ocean. This magma ocean is estimated to have extended to at least several hundred miles (km) in depth. Heavy minerals sank toward the bottom of this magma ocean, while lighter elements floated to the top or were caught in the middle. In this way, the separation and segregation of the heavier metallic elements such as iron (Fe) and nickel (Ni) began. These heavy elements then sank to form the core of the planet, whereas the lighter rocky elements floated upwards to form the crust. This process led to the differentiation or separation of the Earth into several different concentric shells of contrasting density and composition, and was the main control on the large-scale structure of the Earth today.

These main shells of the Earth include the outermost layer called the crust, a light outer shell that is 3–50 miles (5–70 km) thick. This is followed inward by the mantle, a solid rocky layer extending to 1,800 miles (2,900 km) in beneath the surface. The outer core is a molten metallic layer extending to 3,200 miles (5,100 km) in depth and the inner core is a solid metallic layer extending to 3,950 miles (6,370 km) at the center of the Earth.

With the recognition of *plate tectonics* in the 1960s, geologists recognized that the outer parts of the Earth were also divided into several zones that had very different mechanical properties. It was recognized that the outer shell of the Earth was divided into many different rigid plates that are all moving with respect to each other, and some of them carrying continents in continental drift. This outer rigid layer became known as the *lithosphere,* which is the Greek word for "rigid rock sphere." The lithosphere ranges from 45–100 miles (75–150 km) thick. The lithosphere is essentially floating on a denser, but partially molten layer of rock in the upper mantle known as the *asthenosphere* (Greek for "weak sphere"). It is the weakness of this layer that allows the plates on the surface of the Earth to move about.

Physiography: Shape of the Surface of the Planet

The most basic division of the Earth's surface shows that it is divided into continents and ocean basins, with oceans occupying about 60 percent of the surface, and continents 40 percent. A transect, or cross section, across the continent to the ocean shows some major physiographic divisions. Mountains are elevated portions of the continents and form a relatively small area of the surface that is above sea level. Most of the continental area lies below 1,000 feet (300 m) in elevation, with the highest mountains reaching almost 30,000 feet (8,854 m). At the opposite end of the spectrum, the seafloor has a typical depth of 2.5–3 miles (4–5 km), with gradual transitions upwards to shorelines and downwards to some very deep trenches that plunge to depths greater than 36,000 feet (11,040 m). Shorelines are very dynamic areas where the land meets the sea, and are constantly shifting back and forth over geological time in response to changes in the sea level. For instance, the shoreline of the gently sloping Gulf Coast of the United States has shifted offshore and inland by hundreds of miles (km) in response to lowering and rising of sea level in the past 30,000 years, and is presently shifting inland as sea levels rise about one to three feet (0.3–1 m) per century. This shifting of the coastline is often unfortunate for those with expensive beachfront property. Continental shelves are broad to narrow areas underlaid by continental crust, covered by shallow water. Some extend outward hundreds of miles (several hundred km) from the shoreline, until they meet the continental slopes, which are steep drop-offs from the edge of the shelf to the deep ocean basin. These slopes can be so steep that thick piles of loose sediments and rocks sometimes slide and cascade down these slopes all the way to the deep ocean. Continental rises are where the slopes flatten to merge with the deep and dark ocean *abyssal plains* that extend thousands of miles off shore of many continental shelves. Ocean ridge systems such as the Mid-Atlantic Ridge are subaquatic mountain ranges that rise out of the abyssal plains and represent places where new ocean crust is being created by seafloor spreading. These are the most volcanically active areas on Earth. These ridges also experience numerous earthquakes, but most are too small and too far away from any populated landmasses to be felt by people.

Mountain belts on the Earth are of two basic types: orogenic and volcanic. *Orogenic belts* are linear chains of mountains, largely on the continents, that contain highly deformed contorted rocks that represent places where lithospheric plates have collided or slid past one another. The *mid-ocean ridge system* is a 40,000-mile (65,000-km) long mountain ridge that is characterized by vast outpourings of young lava on the ocean floor, and represents places where new oceanic crust is being generated by plate tectonics. After it is formed, it moves away from the ridge crests, and fills the space created by the plates drifting apart. The oceanic basins also contain long, linear, deep ocean trenches that are up to several miles deeper than the surrounding ocean floor. These oceanic trenches locally reach depths of seven miles (11 km) below the sea surface. They represent places where the oceanic crust is sinking back into the mantle of the Earth, completing the plate tectonic cycle for oceanic crust.

Historical Development of the Plate Tectonics Theorem

Geologists and natural philosophers have speculated on the origin of continents, oceans, mountain ranges, and earthquakes for hundreds of years. Early geologists recognized and classified many of the major surface and tectonic features of the continents and oceans. *Cratons* are very old and stable portions of the continents that have been inactive for billions of years, and typically have subdued topography including gentle uplifts and basins. Orogenic belts are long, narrow belts of folded and faulted rocks, and many have frequent volcanic eruptions and earthquakes. Abyssal plains are stable, flat parts of the deep oceanic floor whereas oceanic ridges are mountain ranges beneath the sea with active volcanoes, earthquakes, and high temperatures along their crests. Many early geologists were driven to explain the large-scale tectonic features of the Earth, and proposed many hypotheses, including popular ideas that the Earth was expanding or shrinking, forming ocean basins and mountain ranges. From 1910 to 1925, Alfred Wegener published a prescient and now-classic series of works where he proposed some of the core ideas of the modern plate tectonic concept, especially his 1912 treatise *The Origin of Continents and Oceans.* This book has since been heralded as one of the earliest works that clearly outlined some of the basic ideas that would later form the foundation of the plate tectonics model for the Earth. Wegener proposed that the continents were drifting about on the surface of the planet, and that they once fit together to form one great supercontinent, known as Pangaea. Wegener had many difficulties to overcome to make maps of the coastlines of the different continental masses fit together to form his reconstruction of Pangaea. He defined the continent/ocean transition as the outer edge of the continental shelves to account for continental crust that was thin and resting slightly below sea level. The continental reconstruction proposed by Wegener showed remarkably good fits between coastlines on opposing sides of ocean basins, such as the Brazilian highlands of South America fitting into the Niger delta region of Africa. Wegener's theory of continental drift may be thought of as an early version of plate tectonics, and states that the continents are relatively light objects that are floating and moving freely across a substratum of oceanic crust. The theory was largely discredited because it lacked a driving mechanism, and seemed implausible, if not physically impossible to most geologists at the time, who argued that the relatively weak rocks of continents could not plow through the relatively strong rocks of the ocean floor without being destroyed. Wegener was a meteorologist, and since he was not formally trained as a geologist, few scientists at the time believed in his theory, although current understanding of the Earth suggests that he was largely correct.

Most continental areas, including the central United States, Europe, northern Asia, Africa, and eastern South America lie approximately 985 feet (300 m) above sea level, and if current erosion rates are extrapolated back in time, it is found that continents would be eroded to sea level in 10–15 million years. This observation led geologists to ask why these major continental areas are elevated so high above the heights to which they should be eroded, and then led to the application of the principle

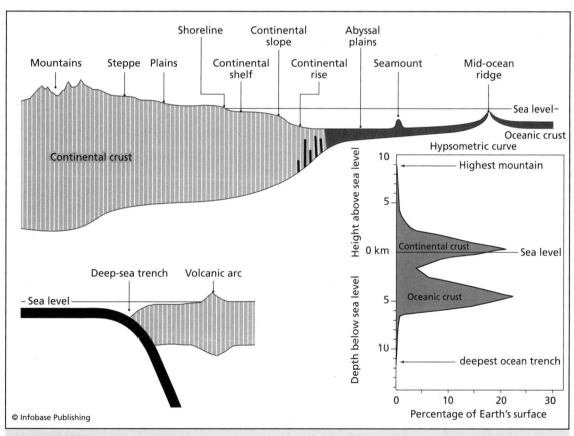

Cross sections of the outer layers of the Earth showing a typical continent to ocean transition (upper) and an oceanic trench to island arc boundary (lower). Inset in box shows the hysometric curve, where the elevation of the land and sea floor are plotted on the vertical axis, and the amount of Earth's surface at each elevation is shown on the horizontal axis. The curve shows that the Earth has two fundamentally different kinds of crust, continental and oceanic, each residing at different elevations

ALFRED LOTHAR WEGENER
(1880–1930)

Alfred Wegener is well known for his studies in meteorology and geophysics and is considered by many to be the father of continental drift. He completed his studies in Berlin and presented a thesis on astronomy. His interest in meteorology and geology led him on a Danish expedition to northeastern Greenland in 1906–08. This was the first of four Greenland expeditions he would make, and this area remained one of his dominant interests.

Wegener studied the apparent correspondence between the shapes of the coastlines of western Africa and eastern South America. Later on he learned that evidence of paleontological similarities was being used to support the theory of the "land bridge" that had connected Brazil to Africa. He continued to study the paleontological and geological evidence and concluded that these similarities demanded an explanation and wrote an extended account of his continental drift theory in his book *Die Entstehung der Kontinente und Ozeane* (*The Origin of Continents and Oceans*). As a meteorologist he began to look at ancient climates, and used paleoclimatic evidence he found to strengthen his theory of continental drift. Wegener was by no means the first think of the theory of continental drift. However, he was the first to go through great lengths to develop and establish the theory. He is also known for his work on dynamics and thermodynamics of the atmosphere, atmospheric refraction and mirages, optical phenomena in clouds, acoustical waves, and the design of geophysical instruments.

of *isostasy* to explain the elevation of the continents. Isostasy, a geological version of Archimedes' Principle, states that continents and high topography are buoyed up by thick continental roots floating in a denser mantle, much like icebergs floating in water. The principle of isostasy states that the elevation of any large segment of crust is directly proportional to the thickness of the crust. Geologists working in Scandinavia in northern Europe noticed that areas that had recently been covered by glaciers were rising quickly relative to sea level, and they equated this important observation with the principle of isostatic rebound. Isostatic rebound is accommodated by the flow of mantle material within the zone of low viscosity (strength) beneath the continental crust, to compensate the rising topography. These observations revealed that mantle material could flow at rates of an inch or two (several cm) per year.

In *The Origin of Continents and Oceans,* Wegener was able to take all the continents and geometrically fit them back together to form a supercontinent, known as Pangaea (or all land), that he suggested existed on Earth 250 million years ago. Wegener also used indicators of paleoclimate, such as locations of ancient deserts and glacial ice sheets, and distributions of certain plant and animal species, to support his ideas. A famous South African geologist, Alexander L. du Toit (1878–1948), who, in 1921, matched the stratigraphy and structure across the Pangaea landmass, supported Wegener's ideas. Du Toit found the same plants, such as a famous seed-fern plant known as *Glossopteris*, across Africa and South America. He also documented similar reptiles and even earthworms across narrow belts of Wegener's Pangaea, supporting the concept of continental drift.

Even with evidence such as the matching of geological belts across Pangaea, most geologists and geophysicists doubted the idea, since it lacked a driving mechanism and it seemed mechanically impossible for

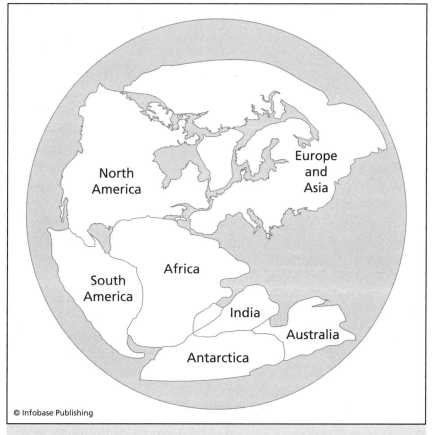

© Infobase Publishing

Map showing the distribution of landmasses in the supercontinent of Pangaea relatively soft continental crust to plow through the much stronger oceanic crust. Early attempts at finding a mechanism were implausible, and included ideas such as tides pushing the continents. Facing a lack of credible, driving mechanisms, continental drift encountered stiff resistance from the geologic community, as few could understand how continents could plow through the mantle.

In 1928, distinguished British geologist Arthur Holmes suggested a driving mechanism for moving the continents. He proposed that heat produced by radioactive decay caused thermal convection in the mantle, and that the laterally flowing mantle dragged the continents with the convection cells. He reasoned that if the mantle can flow to allow isostatic rebound following glaciation, then maybe it can flow laterally as well. The acceptance of thermal convection as a driving mechanism for continental drift represented the foundation of modern plate tectonics. In the 1950s and 1960s, information on the past history of the Earth's magnetic field was collected from many continents, and argued strongly that the continents had indeed been shifting, both with respect to the magnetic pole and also with respect to each other. When seafloor spreading and sinking of oceanic crust beneath island arcs was recognized in the 1960s, the model of continental drift was modified to become the new plate tectonic paradigm that revolutionized and unified many previously diverse fields of the Earth sciences.

In the 1960s, a revolution shook up the Earth sciences that resulted in the acceptance of the plate tectonic model which states that the Earth's outer shell, or lithosphere, is broken into several rigid pieces, called plates, that are all moving with respect to each other. As the plates are rigid, they do not deform internally when they move, but only deform along their edges. Therefore most of the world's earthquakes and active volcanoes are located along plate boundaries, and this is where most mountain belts are formed. The plates are moving as a response to heating of the mantle by radioactive decay, and are in many ways analogous to ice layers floating on the surface of a lake during spring break-up. Where the ice moves apart, new water upwells to fill the void, where the ice converges the edges of the sheets are deformed, and in still other places the ice simply slides past adjacent sheets. Likewise, where the plates collide, earthquakes occur and mountains form, and where they move apart, new ocean basins are formed.

Since plates do not deform internally, most of the earthquakes, faulting and folding, and volcanic action happens along their edges. Geometrically there are only three fundamental types of plate bound-

ALEXANDER LOGIE DU TOIT
(1878–1948)

Alexander du Toit is known as "the world's greatest field geologist." He was born near Cape Town and went to school at a local diocesan college. He then graduated from South Africa College and then spent two years studying mining engineering at the Royal Technical College in Glasgow, and geology at the Royal College of Science in London. In 1901, he was a lecturer at the Royal Technical College and at the University of Glasgow. He returned to South Africa in 1903, joining the Geological Commission of the Cape of Good Hope and spent the next several years constantly in the field doing geological mapping. This time in his life was the foundation for his extensive understanding and unrivaled knowledge South African geology.

During his first season, he worked with Arthur W. Rogers in the western Karoo where they established the stratigraphy of the Lower and Middle Karoo System. They also recorded the systematic phase changes in the Karoo and Cape Systems. Along with these studies they mapped the dolerite intrusives, their acid phases, and their metamorphic aureoles. Throughout the years, du Toit worked in many areas including the Stormberg area and the Karoo coal deposits near the Indian Ocean. He was very interested in geomorphology and hydrogeology. The most significant factor to his work was the theory of continental drift. He was the first to realize that the southern continents had once formed the supercontinent of Gondwana that was distinctly different from the northern supercontinent Laurasia. Du Toit received many honors and awards. He was the president of the Geological Society of South Africa, a corresponding member of the Geological Society of America, and a member of the Royal Society of London.

aries. *Divergent boundaries* are where two plates move apart, creating a void that is typically filled by new oceanic crust that wells up to fill the progressively opening hole. *Convergent boundaries* are where two plates move toward each other, resulting in one plate sliding beneath the other when a dense oceanic plate is involved, or collision and deformation, when continental plates are involved. These types of plate boundaries may have the largest of all earthquakes. *Transform boundaries* form where two plates slide past each other, such as along the San Andreas Fault in California, and may also result in large earthquakes.

Since all plates are moving with respect to each other, the surface of the Earth is made up of a mosaic of various plate boundaries, and the geologist has an amazing diversity of different geological environments to study. Every time one plate moves, the others must move to accommodate this motion, creating a never-ending saga of different plate configurations. This ever-changing arrangement of plates causes earthquakes, volcanic eruptions, uplift of mountains (with landslides), and influences global atmospheric patterns. Therefore, the arrangement of the plates helps determine which areas have monsoonal floods, which have earthquakes, and which tend to be stable.

Where plates diverge, seafloor spreading produces new oceanic crust, as volcanic *basalt* pours out of the depths of the Earth, filling the gaps generated by the moving plates. Examples of where this can be seen on the surface include Iceland along the Reykjanes Ridge. Beneath the Rekjanes and other oceanic ridges, magma rises from depth in the mantle and forms chambers filled with magma just below the crest of the ridges. The magma in these chambers erupts out through cracks in the roof of the chambers, and forms extensive lava flows on the surface. As the two different plates on either side of the magma chamber move apart, these lava flows continuously fill in the gap between the diverging plates, creating new oceanic crust.

Oceanic lithosphere is being destroyed by sinking back into the mantle at the deep ocean trenches, in a process called *subduction.* As the oceanic slabs go down, they experience higher temperatures that cause rock-melts or magmas to be generated, which then move upwards to intrude the overlying plate. Since subduction zones are long, narrow zones where large plates are being withdrawn into the mantle, the melting produces a long line of volcanoes above the down-going plate and forms a volcanic arc. Depending on what the overriding plate is made of, this arc may be built on either a continental or on an oceanic plate.

Plate tectonics and tectonic boundaries are extremely important for understanding geologic hazards, in that most of the planet's earthquakes, volcanic eruptions, and other hazards are located along and directly created by the interaction of plates, and the concentration of economic minerals (including petroleum) is controlled by the plate tectonic setting. An understanding of plate tectonics is therefore essential for planning for geologic hazards, and for locating strategic mineral resources.

Plate Tectonics and the Hazardous Earth

Plate tectonics can be thought of as the surface expression of energy loss from deep within the Earth. With so much energy loss accommodated by plate tectonics, we can expect that plate tectonics is one of the major energy sources for natural disasters and hazards, including earthquakes. Most of the earthquakes on the planet are directly associated with plate boundaries and these sometimes devastating events account for much of the motion between the plates. Individual earthquakes have killed tens and even hundreds of thousands of people, such as the 1976 Tang Shan earthquake in China that killed a quarter million people and the 2004 Sumatra earthquake and tsunami that killed an estimated 283,000 people. Earthquakes also cause enormous financial and insurance losses. For instance, the 1994 Northridge earthquake in California caused more than $14 billion in losses. Most of the world's volcanoes are also associated with plate boundaries. Thousands of volcanic vents are located along the mid-ocean ridge system, and most of the volume of magma produced on the Earth is erupted through these volcanoes. Volcanism associated with the mid-ocean ridge system is, however, rarely explosive, hazardous, or even noticed by humans. Volcanoes that are situated above subduction zones at convergent boundaries are, in contrast, capable of producing tremendous explosive eruptions, with great devastation of local regions. Volcanic eruptions and associated phenomena have killed tens of thousands of people the 20th century, including the massive mudslides at Nevado del Ruiz in Colombia that killed 23,000 in 1985. Some of the larger volcanic eruptions cover huge parts of the globe with volcanic ash and are capable of changing the global climate. Some places in the United States appear almost ready to produce huge volcanic eruptions, such as Yellowstone National Park and the Mammoth Lakes of California. Plate tectonics is also responsible for uplifting the world's mountain belts that are associated with their own sets of hazards, particularly landslides and other *mass wasting* phenomena.

How Plate Tectonics Works

Plate tectonics is the study of the large-scale evolution of the lithosphere of the Earth. In the 1960s, the Earth sciences experienced a scientific revolution, when the model of plate tectonics was formulated from a number of previous hypotheses that attempted to explain different aspects about the evolution of continents, oceans, and mountain belts. New plate material is created at mid-ocean ridges and destroyed when it sinks back into the mantle in deep-sea trenches. Scientists had known for some time that the Earth is divided into many layers defined mostly by chemical characteristics, including the inner core, outer core, mantle, and crust. The plate tectonic paradigm led to the under-standing that the Earth is also divided mechanically, and includes a rigid outer layer, called the lithosphere, sitting upon a very weak layer containing a small amount of partial melt of *peridotite*, termed the asthenosphere. The lithosphere is about 75 miles (125 km) thick under continents, and 45 miles (75 km) thick under oceans, whereas the asthenosphere extends to about 155 miles (250 km) in depth. The basic theorem of plate tectonics is that the outer shell or lithosphere of the Earth is broken into about twelve large rigid blocks or plates that are all moving relative to one another. Smaller plates fill in the gaps between the larger plates. These plates are rotationally rigid, meaning that they can rotate about on the surface and not deform significantly internally. Most deformation of plates, and earthquakes, occurs along their edges, where they interact with other plates.

Plate tectonics has been a unifying science, bringing together diverse fields such as structural geology (study of the deformation of rocks), geophysics (study of the physical properties of Earth), sedimentology and stratigraphy (studies of sediments and sedimentary rocks), paleon-tology (history of life on Earth), geochronology (relative and absolute ages of rocks and minerals), and geomorphology (study of land surface features), especially with respect to active tectonics (also known as neo-tectonics). Plate motion almost always involves the melting of rocks, so other fields are also important, including igneous petrology (study of formation of rocks from magma), metamorphic petrology (study of the changes in rocks from heat and pressure), and geochemistry (study of the chemical composition of rocks).

The base of the crust, known as the *Mohorovicic discontinuity* (or simply the Moho), is defined with earthquake or seismic waves, and reflects the difference in seismic velocities of the crust, composed of relatively light basalt, and the mantle, composed of denser peridotite. However, the base of the lithosphere is defined as where the same rock type on either side begins to melt, and it corresponds roughly to a place where the temperature reaches 2,425°F (1,330°C) at depth. The main rock types of interest to tectonics include *granite, granodiorite,* basalt, and peridotite. The average continental crustal composition is equivalent to granodiorite (the density of granodiorite is 2.6 g/cm^3; its mineralogy includes quartz, plagioclase, biotite, and some potassium feldspar). The average oceanic crustal composition is equivalent to that of basalt (the density of basalt is 3.0 g/cm^3; its mineralogy includes pla-gioclase, clinopyroxene, and olivine). The average upper mantle composition is equivalent to peridotite (the density of peridotite is 3.3 g/cm³; its mineralogy includes olivine, clinopyroxene, and orthopyroxene). Considering the densities of these rock types, the crust can be thought of as floating on the mantle; mechanically, the lithosphere floats on the asthenosphere.

The movement of plates on the spherical Earth can be described by a rotation about a pole of rotation, using a mathematical theorem first described by Leonhard Euler in 1776. Euler's theorem states that any movement of a spherical plate over a spherical surface can be described by a rotation about an axis (like a pin piercing a ball of clay) that passes through the center of the sphere. The place where the axis of rotation passes through the surface of the Earth is referred to as the *pole of rotation.* The pole of rotation can be thought of as analogous to the pivot point of a pair of scissors opening and closing, but curved around the surface of the Earth. The motions of one side of the scissors can be described as a rotation of the other side about the

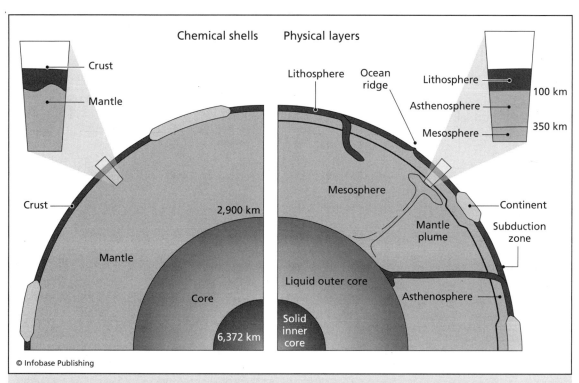

Cross sections of the Earth showing chemical shells (crust, mantle, and core) and physical layers (lithosphere, asthenosphere, mesosphere, outer core, and inner core)

	Felsic	Intermediate		Mafic	Ultramafic
Plutonic	Granite	Granodiorite	Diorite	Gabbro	Peridotite
Volcanic	Rhyolite	Dacite	Andesite	Basalt	Komatiite
	Light colored				Dark colored

← Increasing silica (SiO₂)

© Infobase Publishing

Igneous rock classification scheme based on the amount of silica (SiO$_2$) in a rock and its texture. Plutonic rocks are generally coarse grained whereas volcanic rocks are generally fine grained.

pin, either opening or closing the blades of the scissors. The motion of plates about a pole of rotation is expressed using an *angular velocity*. As the plates rotate, locations near the pole of rotation experience low angular velocities, whereas points on the same plates that are far from the pole of rotation experience much greater angular velocities.

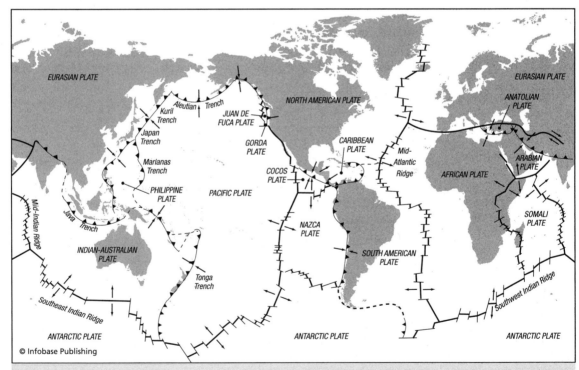

© Infobase Publishing

Map of the Earth showing the major divergent, convergent, and transform plate boundaries and outlines of the continents

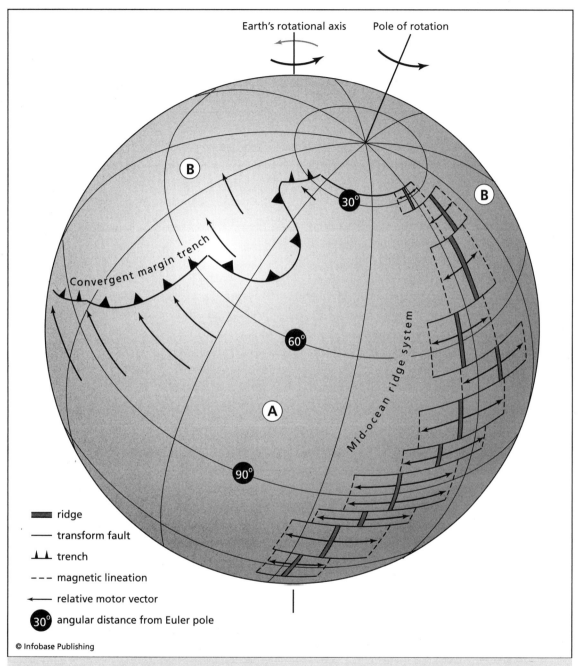

Pole of rotation on a sphere. Plate A rotates away from plate B, with ridge axes falling on great circles intersecting at the pole of rotation, and oceanic transform faults falling along small circles that are concentric about the pole of rotation. The angular velocity of the plate increases with increasing distance from the pole of rotation.

Oceanic spreading rates or convergence rates along subduction zones may vary greatly along a single plate boundary. This type of relationship is similar to a marching band going around a corner. The musicians near the corner have to march in place and pivot (acting as a pole of rotation) while the musicians on the outside of the corner need to march quickly to keep the lines in the band formation straight as they go around the corner.

Rotations of plates on the Earth lead to some interesting geometrical consequences for plate tectonics. We find that mid-ocean ridges are oriented so that the ridge axes all point toward the pole of rotation, and are aligned on great circles that pass through the pole of rotation. Transform faults lie on small circles that are concentric around the pole of rotation. In contrast, convergent boundaries may lie at any angle with respect to poles of rotation.

Since all plates are moving with respect to each other, the surface of the Earth is made up of a mosaic of various plate boundaries, and the geologist has an amazing diversity of different geological environments to study. Every time one plate moves, the others must move to accommodate this motion, creating a never-ending saga of different plate configurations.

Conclusion

This chapter discussed how the different major landforms on the surface of the Earth are related to plate tectonics and geological hazards. The model of plate tectonics describes how the surface layer of the Earth, known as the lithosphere, is divided into more than a dozen rigid plates that are all moving at rates of up to a few inches (several cm) per year. Motion along the edges of the plates causes earthquakes, and deformation such as folding and faulting along these edges forms mountain belts. Plates may have three kinds of boundaries with other plates: divergent, convergent, or transform. At divergent boundaries two plates are moving apart and new material, generally molten magma, moves up from the mantle to fill in the gap forming new plate material. At transform boundaries, such as the San Andreas Fault in California, two plates are sliding past each other and may generate many earthquakes. The most complex type of plate boundaries are convergent boundaries, where one plate may slide under another in a subduction zone, partly melting at depth. Where the magmas rise a volcanic arc is formed on the surface. In other places, two plates collide forming huge mountain ranges like the Himalaya. Thus, convergent plate boundaries are characterized by tall mountains, active volcanism, and active faulting, and are among the most hazardous places to live because of the diverse set of geological hazards.

2

Divergent Plate Boundaries

W here plates move apart or diverge, continents are torn into pieces, resulting in spreading of the seafloor, which eventually produces new oceanic crust. This section examines the different types of divergent or extensional plate boundaries, and the processes that are active along them. These processes are illustrated with detailed examination of a few of the world's best examples of each main process, including a place called the Afar depression in northeastern Africa where the African continent is being ripped apart along an extensional plate boundary. Other branches of the boundary here have evolved into oceanic spreading centers in the Red Sea and the Gulf of Aden, where Arabia has separated from Africa. In another example of a divergent plate boundary, the island of Iceland in the northern Atlantic Ocean is shown to be a place where an oceanic spreading center rises above sea level exposing rocks and processes that are normally only observable in the deep ocean.

Divergent Plate Boundary Processes

The world's longest mountain chain is the mid-ocean ridge system, extending 25,000 miles (40,000 km) around the planet through all the major oceans of the world. The mid-ocean ridge system represents places where two plates are moving apart or diverging, and new material is upwelling from the mantle to form new oceanic crust and lithosphere. These mid-ocean ridge systems are mature extensional boundaries, many of which began as immature extensional boundaries in continents, known as continental rifts. Some continental rift systems are linked to the world rift system in the oceans and are actively breaking continents into pieces. An example is the Red Sea–East African rift system. Other continental rifts are accommodating small amounts of extension in the crust, and may never evolve into oceanic rifts. Examples of where this type of rifting occurs on a large scale include the Basin and Range Province of the western United States, and Lake Baikal in Siberia.

Divergent Plate Boundaries in Continents

Rifts are elongate depressions formed where the entire thickness of the lithosphere has ruptured in extension. These are places where the continents are beginning to break apart, and if successful, may form new ocean basins. The general geomorphic feature that initially forms is known as a rift valley. Rift valleys have steep, fault-bounded sides, with rift shoulders that typically tilt slightly away from the rift valley floor. Examples of this kind of topography are common in the East African rift system, where rivers on the uplifted margins flow away from the internal valley because the rift shoulders are tilted away from that valley. Drainage systems within rifts tend to be short, internal systems, with streams forming on the steep escarpments dropping into the rift, flowing along the rift axis, and draining into deep, narrow lakes within the rift. If the rift is in an arid environment, such as much of East Africa, the drainage may have no outlet and the water will evaporate before it can reach the sea. Such evaporation leaves distinctive deposits of salts and other minerals that form by being left behind during evaporation of sea water (evaporites), one of the hallmark deposits of continental rift settings. Other types of deposits in rifts include lake sediments in rift centers, and conglomerates (cemented gravels) derived from rocks exposed along the rift shoulders. Conglomerates are common next to many of the steep escarpments in the East African rift, such as those near Lakes Tanganyika, Edward, and Albert between Zaire, Tanzania, Burundi, and Rwanda. These sediments may be interleaved with volcanic rocks, are typically alkaline (having abundant sodium [Na] and other alkali elements) in character and bimodal in silica content (i.e., basalts and rhyolites).

When continents break up to form oceans, they do so by forming a three-armed rift system known as a triple junction. When two arms of these triple junctions successfully spread apart to form an ocean, they leave one arm of the triple junction behind jutting into the interior of the continent, along with marginal fault systems and thick accumulations of sediments. Many of the world's major rivers, including the Mississippi, Hudson, Amazon, and Congo, follow failed arms of triple junctions. These failed arms are associated with deep-seated fault systems that may occasionally be activated by stresses in the interior of continents. Perhaps the most famous earthquakes associated with a failed arm of a rift are the 1811 and 1812 earthquakes on the New Madrid fault of the central United States. These earthquakes included a series of severe events, including three magnitude 7.5–8.0 events that could be felt across the nation.

KEVIN C. BURKE
(1929–   )

Born in London, England, November 13, 1929, Burke lived there until the age of 23, taking bachelor's and doctoral degrees at University College, London. The latter degree involved field mapping of crystalline rocks in Galway, Ireland. In 1953, Burke was appointed a lecturer at what is now the University of Ghana and, apart from five years working with the British Geological Survey (1956-61), he spent the next 20 years teaching and doing field-related research at universities in Ghana, Korea, Jamaica, Nigeria, and Canada. In Canada he spent two years working with Tuzo Wilson at the University of Toronto and in 1973 he joined the geology department at SUNY Albany, where he spent 10 years working mainly with John Dewey, Bill Kidd, and Celal Sengor on a variety of tectonic problems. This group formulated tectonic models for many of the world's basins and mountain belts, and made reconstructions of the continents at various times in Earth history. In 1983, Burke was appointed professor at the University of Houston, between 1983 and 1988 serving as Director of the Lunar and Planetary Institute in Clear Lake. Between 1989 and 1992 Burke worked at the National Research Council in Washington with scientists putting together a major report on the future of the solid earth sciences.

Burke has focused many of his efforts on Africa, especially on the processes of continental rifting, although he publishes extensively on other parts of the world especially Asia and the Caribbean. Burke has devoted great efforts to editing journals and to national and international committees. He is founding editor of the *Journal of Asian Earth Sciences* and was the president of the Scientific Committee on the Lithosphere of the International Council of Scientific Unions.

Modes of Extension

Although divergent boundaries are all similar in that they are places where the crust and entire lithosphere are breaking and moving apart, there are large differences in the processes that allow this extension to occur. Some of these different processes act in different places, others may work together to produce the extension and associated sinking (subsidence) of the land surface. There are three main end-member models for the mechanisms of extension and subsidence in continental rifts. These are the pure shear model, the simple shear model, and the dike injection model.

In the pure shear model for extension, the lithosphere thins symmetrically about the rift axis, being pulled apart like taffy at depth, and along brittle faults near the surface. The base of the lithosphere (defined by the 2,425°F [1,330°C] isotherm or line of equal temperature) rises to 10–20 miles (15–30 km) below the surface near the center of the rift axis but remains at normal depths of 75 miles (120 km) away from the rift. This causes high heat flow and high temperature gradients with depth (geothermal gradients) in rifts, and is consistent with many measurements of the strength of the Earth's gravity force, that suggest an excess mass at depth (this would correspond to the denser asthenosphere near the surface). Stretching mechanisms in the pure shear model include brittle accommodation of stretching on faults near the surface. At about four miles (7 km) depth, the rocks stop to deform by fracturing, and begin to flow like silly putty—this transition is known as the brittle ductile transition, and extension below this depth is accommodated by shear on ductile shear zones.

In the simple shear model for extension, an asymmetric fault known as a detachment fault penetrates the thickness of the lithosphere, dipping a few degrees forming a system of asymmetric structures across the rift. A series of rotated fault blocks may form where the detachment is close to the surface, whereas the opposite side of the rift (where the lithosphere experiences the most thinning) may be dominated by the eruption of volcanic rocks. Heating of the crust associated with the lithospheric thinning typically causes the upward doming of the detachment fault, and since the heating (and uplift) is greatest in a region offset from the center of the rifting zone, the center of the uplifted dome tends to be located on one side of the rift. This model explains differences on either side of rifts, such as faulted and volcanic margins now on opposite continental margins (conjugate margins) of former rifts that have evolved into oceans. A good example of where this can be observed is

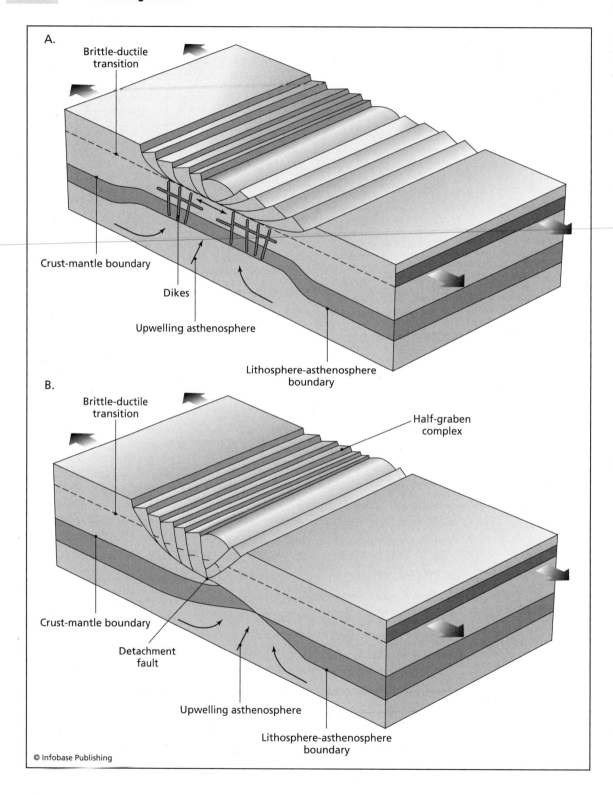

A.

Brittle-ductile
transition

Crust-mantle boundary

Dikes

Upwelling asthenosphere

Lithosphere-asthenosphere
boundary

B.

Brittle-ductile
transition

Half-graben
complex

Crust-mantle boundary

Detachment
fault

Upwelling asthenosphere

Lithosphere-asthenosphere
boundary

© Infobase Publishing

(opposite page) Modes of extension in rifts. Pure shear model (A) in which the lithosphere extends asymmetrically, and the asthenosphere rises to fill the space vacated by the extending lithosphere. Simple shear or asymmetric rifting (B) where a shallow dipping detachment fault penetrates the thickness of the lithosphere, and the asthenosphere rises asymmetrically on the side of the rift where the fault enters the asthenosphere. Faulting patterns are also asymmetric, with different styles on either side of the rift.

along the Red Sea of the Middle East, where many volcanic rocks are located on the Arabian side of the sea, and few are found on the African side of the rift.

The dike injection model for extension for rifts suggests that a large number of dense igneous dikes (with basaltic composition) intrude the continental lithosphere in rifts, causing the lithosphere to become denser and to sink or subside. This mechanism does not really explain most aspects of rifts, but it may contribute to the total amount of subsidence in the other two models.

In all of these models for initial extension of the rift, initial geothermal gradients (how the temperature changes with depth) are raised and the temperatures become elevated and compressed beneath the rift axis. After the initial stretching and subsidence phases, the rift either becomes inactive or evolves into a mid-ocean ridge system. In the latter case, the initial shoulders of the rift become passive continental margins. Failed rifts and passive continental margins both enter a second, slower phase of subsidence related to the gradual recovery of the isotherms (lines of equal temperature) to their deeper, prerifting levels. This process takes about 60 million years, and typically forms a broad basin over the initial rifts, characterized by no active faults, no volcanism, and rare lakes. The transition from initial stretching with coarse, clastic (made up of preexisting rocks) sediments and volcanics to the thermal subsidence phase is commonly called the "rift to drift" transition on passive margins.

Divergent Plate Boundaries in the Oceans

Some continental rifts may evolve into mid-ocean ridge spreading centers. The world's best example of where this transition can be observed is in the Ethiopian Afar, where the East African continental rift system meets juvenile oceanic spreading centers in the Red Sea and Gulf of Aden as described in the sidebar on page 26, "Transition from Continental to Oceanic Rifting: The Afar Triangle." Three plate boundaries meet in a wide plate boundary zone in the Afar, including the African/Arabian boundary (Red Sea spreading center), the Arabian/Somalian boundary (Gulf of Aden spreading center), and the African/Somalian boundary (East African rift). The boundary is a complex system known as a RRR (rift-rift-rift) *triple junction.* The triple junction has many complex extensional structures, with most of the Afar near sea level, and isolated blocks of continental crust such as the Danakil Horst isolated from the rest of the continental crust by normal faults.

The Red Sea has a young or juvenile spreading center similar in some aspects to the spreading center in the middle of the Atlantic Ocean. Geologists recognize two main classes of oceanic spreading centers,

TRANSITION FROM CONTINENTAL TO OCEANIC RIFTING: THE AFAR TRIANGLE

The Afar depression, Ethiopia, is one of the world's largest, deepest regions below sea level that is exposed to the atmosphere on the continents, and is home to some of the earliest known hominid fossils. The Afar is a hot, arid region, where the Awash River drains northward out of the East African rift system, and is evaporated in Lake Abhe before a single drop of water ever reaches the sea. It is located in eastern Africa in Ethiopia and Eritrea, between Sudan, Somalia, and across the Red Sea and Gulf of Aden from Yemen. The reason the region is so topographically low is that it is located at a tectonic triple junction, where three main extensional plate boundaries that are all spreading apart meet, forming three intersecting rifts, causing regional sub-

A triple junction where three plates meet at one place, is exposed where three extensional rifts meet in the Afar triangle of Ethiopia. Satellite image shows the East African Rift meeting the Red Sea and Gulf of Aden Rifts. Dashed lines show approximate boundaries between the African plate (on the west) and the Somali plate (on the east), with the East African rift valley forming the lowlands between the dashed lines. Bold arrows indicate the direction of movement of the Somali and Arabian plates away from Africa. *(T. Kusky)*

sidence, or sinking of the land. These three intersecting rifts include one extending southwest from the Afar to the interior of the African continent, one extending northwest from the Afar into the Red Sea, and one extending northeast into the Gulf of Aden.

Atlantic-type and Pacific-type, based on characteristics of the shapes of their surfaces (geomorphology) and elevation or topography. These different types are formed in spreading centers with different spreading rates—with slow spreading rates, 0.2–0.8 inches per year (0.5–2 cm/yr), on Atlantic-type ridges, and faster rates, generally 1.5–3.5 inches per year (4–9 cm/yr), on Pacific-type ridges.

Atlantic-type ridges are characterized by a broad, 900–2,000-mile (1,500–3,000-km) wide swell in which the seafloor rises 0.6–1.8 miles (1–3 km) from abyssal plains at 2.5 miles (4.0 km) below sea level to about 1.7 miles (2.8 km) below sea level along the ridge axis. Slopes on the ridge are generally less than 1°. Slow or Atlantic-type ridges have

The Arabian plate is moving northeast away from the African plate, and the Somali plate is moving, at a much slower rate, to the southeast away from Africa. The southern Red Sea and north-central Afar depression form two parallel north–northwest-trending rift basins, separated by the Danakil Horst (an elevated fault block), related to the separation of Arabia from Africa. Of the two rifts, the Afar depression is exposed at the surface, whereas the Red Sea rift floor is submerged below the sea. The Afar triple junction is complex, consisting of many elevated and sunken fault blocks called horsts and grabens, developed on massive volcanic flows. The Afar depression merges southward with the northeast-striking Main Ethiopian Rift, and eastward with the east-northeast-striking Gulf of Aden. The Ethiopian plateau bounds it on the west. Very young volcanic rocks occupy the floor of the Afar depression, and recent clastic and chemical sediments are interlayered with the volcanics in the basins.

The Main Ethiopian and north-central Afar rifts are part of the continental East African Rift System. These two distinct rift systems, typical of intracontinental rifting, are at different stages of evolution. In the north and east, the continental rifts meet the oceanic rifts of the Red Sea and Gulf of Aden, respectively, both of which have propagated into the continent. Geophysical studies indicate that the thickness of the crust in the Main Ethiopian Rift is less than or equal to 18 miles (30 km). In Afar the thickness varies from 14–16 miles (23–26 km) in the south to eight miles (14 km) in the north. The plateau on both sides of the rift has a crustal thickness of 21–27 miles (35–44 km). Rates of separation obtained from geologic and geodetic studies indicate 0.1–0.2 inches (3–6 mm) per year across the northern sector of the Main Ethiopian Rift between the African and Somali plates. The rate of spreading between Africa and Arabia across the north–central Afar rift is relatively faster, about 0.8 inches (2 cm) per year. Paleomagnetic directions from Cenozoic basalts on the Arabian side of the Gulf of Aden indicate seven degrees of counterclockwise rotation of the Arabian plate relative to Africa, and clockwise rotations of up to 11 degrees for blocks in eastern Afar. The initiation of extension on both sides of the southernmost Red Sea Rift, Ethiopia, and Yemen appear to be nearly identical, with extension starting between 22 and 29 million years ago.

a median rift, typically about 20 miles (30 km) wide at the top to 0.6–2.5 miles (1–4 km) wide at the bottom of the long deep medial rift. Many constructional volcanoes are located along the base and inner wall of the medial rift. Rugged topography and many faults forming a strongly block-faulted slope characterize the central part of Atlantic-type ridges.

Pacific-type ridges are generally 1,250–2,500 miles (2,000–4,000 km) wide, and rise 1.2–1.8 miles (2–3 km) above the abyssal plains, with 0.1° slopes. Pacific-type ridges have no median valley, but have many shallow earthquakes, high heat flow, and low gravity in the center of the ridge, suggesting that magma may be present at shallow levels beneath the surface. Pacific-type ridges have much smoother flanks than Atlantic-type ridges.

The high topography of both types of ridges shows that there is underlying low-density material and they are floating on this hot substrate. Geologists call this mechanism of making mountains isostatic compensation. New magma upwells beneath the ridges and forms small magma chambers along the ridge axis. The magma in these chambers crystallizes to form the rocks of the oceanic crust that gets added (in approximately equal proportions) to both diverging plates. The young crust formed at the ridges is hot and relatively light, so it floats on the hot, underlying asthenosphere. As the crust ages and moves away from the ridge it becomes thicker and denser, and subsides, explaining the topographic profile of the ridges. The rate of thermal subsidence is the same for fast-and slow-spreading ridges (a function of the square root of the age of the crust), explaining why slow-spreading ridges are narrower than fast-spreading ridges.

Abundant volcanoes, with vast outpourings of basaltic lava, characterize the centers of the mid-ocean ridges. The lavas are typically bulbous-shaped forms called *pillow lava,* as well as tubes and other more massive flows. The ridge axes are also characterized by very high heat flow, with many thermal vents marking places where seawater has infiltrated the oceanic crust, and made its way to deeper levels where it is heated by coming close to the magma, then rises again to vent on the seafloor. Many of these vents precipitate sulfide and other minerals in great quantities, forming chimneys called "black smokers" that may be many tens of feet tall. These chimneys have high-temperature metal- and nutrient-rich water flowing out of them (at temperatures of several hundred degrees Celsius), with the metals precipitating once the temperature drops upon contact with the cold seawater outside the vent.

These systems may cover parts of the oceanic crust with layers of sulfide minerals. Unusual primitive communities of sulfide-reducing bacteria, tube worms, and crabs have been found near several black smoker vents along mid-ocean ridges. Many scientists believe that similar settings may have played an important role in the early appearance and evolution of life on the planet.

Geophysical seismic refraction studies in the 1940s and 1950s established that the oceanic crust exhibits seismic layering that is similar in many places in the oceans. Seismic layer 1 consists of sediments, layer 2 is interpreted to be a layer of basalt 0.6–1.5 miles (1–2.5 km) thick, and layer 3 is approximately four miles (6 km) thick and interpreted to be crystal cumulates, underlain by the mantle. Some ridges and transform faults expose deeper levels of the oceanic lithosphere, which can be shown to typically include a *mafic* dike complex, thick sections of gabbro (coarse-grained igneous rock), and ultramafic cumulates. In some places, rocks of the underlying mantle are exposed, typically consisting of strongly deformed ultramafic rocks that have had a large amount of magma squeezed out of them. These unusual rocks are called depleted harzburgite tectonites.

As the plates move apart, the pressure on deep underlying rocks is lowered, which causes them to rise and partially melt by 15–25 percent. Basaltic magma is produced by partially melting the peridotitic mantle, removing the melt to form the magma that moves upward to form the oceanic crust, and leaving a "residue" type of rock (harzburgite) in the mantle. The magma produced in this way moves up from deep within the mantle to fill the gap opened by the diverging plates. This magma forms a chamber of molten or partially molten rock that slowly crystallizes to form gabbro, which has the same composition as basalt. Before crystallization, some of the magma moves up to the surface through a series of dikes and forms the crustal sheeted dike complex, and basaltic flows. Many of the basaltic flows have distinctive forms with the magma forming bulbous lobes known as pillow lavas. Lava tubes are also common, as are fragmented pillows formed by the inward explosive collapse (implosion) of the lava tubes and pillows. Back in the magma chamber, other crystals grow in the gabbroic magma, including olivine and pyroxene, which are heavier than the magma and sink to the bottom of the chamber. These crystals form layers of dense minerals known as cumulates. Beneath the cumulates, the mantle material from which the magma was derived gets progressively more deformed as the plates diverge, and form a highly deformed

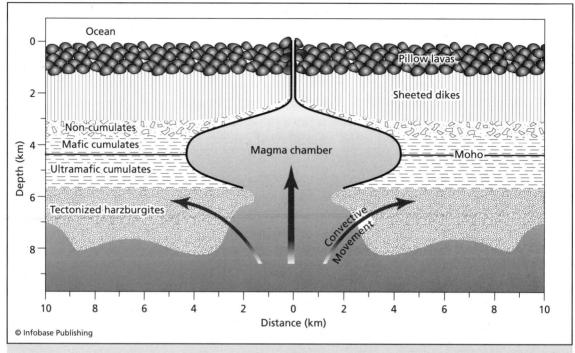

Ocean

Pillow lavas

Sheeted dikes

Non-cumulates
Mafic cumulates

Magma chamber

Moho

Ultramafic cumulates

Tectonized harzburgites

Convective Movement

Depth (km)

Distance (km)

© Infobase Publishing

Formation of oceanic crust at mid-ocean spreading ridges. Magma forms by partial melting in the asthenosphere and upwells to form a magma chamber beneath the ridge axis. As the plates move apart, dikes intrude upward from the magma chamber and feed lava flows on the surface. Heavy crystals settle out of the magma chamber and form layers of crystal cumulates on the magma chamber floor.

ultramafic rock known as a harzburgite or mantle tectonite. This process can be seen on the surface in Iceland along the Reykjanes Ridge.

Much of the detailed information about the deep structure of oceanic crust comes from the study of ophiolites, which are interpreted to be on-land equivalents of oceanic crust tectonically emplaced on the continents during the process of convergent tectonics and ocean closure. Studies of ophiolites have confirmed the general structure of the oceanic crust as inferred from the seismic reflection and refraction studies and limited drilling. Numerous detailed studies of ophiolites have allowed unprecedented detail about the structure and chemistry of inferred oceanic crust and lithosphere to be completed, and as many variations as similarities have been discovered. The causes of these variations are numerous, including differences in spreading rate, magma supply, temperature, depth of melting, tectonic setting (arc, forearc, backarc, mid-ocean ridge), and the presence or absence of water. The ocean floor is, however, still largely unexplored, and we know more about many other planetary surfaces than we know about the ocean floor of the Earth.

The Mid-Atlantic Ridge rises above sea level on the North Atlantic island of Iceland, lying 178 miles (285 km) off the coast of Greenland and 495 miles (792 km) from the coast of Scotland. Iceland has an average elevation of more than 1,600 feet (500 m), and owes its elevation to a *hot spot* that is interacting with the mid-ocean ridge system beneath the island. The Mid-Atlantic Ridge crosses the island from southwest to northeast, and has a spreading rate of 1.2 inches per year (3 cm/yr) with the mean extension oriented toward an azimuth of 103°. The oceanic Reykjanes Ridge and sinistral transform south of the island rise to the surface and continue as the Western Rift zone. Active spreading is transferred to the Southern Volcanic zone across a transform fault called the South Iceland Seismic zone, then continues north through the Eastern Rift zone. Spreading is offset from the oceanic Kolbeinsey ridge by the dextral Tjornes fracture zone off the island's northern coast.

During the past 6 million years, the Iceland hot spot has drifted toward the southeast relative to the North Atlantic, and the oceanic ridge system has made a succession of small jumps so that active spreading has remained coincident with the plume of hottest, weakest

Satellite image of mid-ocean ridge exposed on Iceland. The ridge system strikes into Iceland in the western rift zone and southern volcanic zone in the south, and along the eastern rift zone in the north. *(T. Kusky)*

mantle material. These ridge jumps have caused the active spreading to propagate into regions of older crust that have been remelted, forming unusual alkalic and even silicic volcanic rocks that are deposited unconformably over older oceanic (tholeiitic) basalts. Active spreading occurs along a series of 5–60 mile (10–100 km) long zones of fissures, graben, and dike swarms, with basaltic and rhyolitic volcanoes rising from central parts of fissures. *Hydrothermal* activity is intense along the fracture zones with diffuse faulting and volcanic activity merging into a narrow zone within a few miles beneath the surface. Detailed geophysical studies have shown that magma episodically rises from depth into magma chambers located a few miles below the surface, then dikes intrude the overlying crust and flow horizontally for tens of miles to accommodate crustal extension of several tens of feet over several hundred years.

Many Holocene volcanic events are known from Iceland including 17 eruptions of Hekla from the Southern volcanic zone. Iceland has an extensive system of glaciers, and has experienced a number of eruptions beneath the glaciers that cause water to infiltrate the fracture zones. The mixture of water and magma induces explosive events including *Plinian* eruption clouds, phreo-magmatic, *tephra*-producing eruptions, and sudden floods known as jokulhlaups, induced when the glacier experiences rapid melting from contact with magma. Many Icelanders have learned to use the high geothermal gradients to extract geothermal energy for heating, and to enjoy the many hot springs on the island.

Conclusion

Divergent plate boundaries are places where two tectonic plates are moving apart from each other, forming a long deep valley known as a rift in between the two plates. Some divergent plate boundaries cut through continents and form steep-sided rifts with many deep lakes, active volcanoes, and small earthquakes. The best known divergent plate boundary with a good rift system associated with it is the East African rift system, where the eastern part of Africa is starting to move away from the rest of Africa. The northern part of the East African rift merges into a more evolved divergent plate boundary, where the continental block of Arabia has moved away from Africa so much that rocks from the mantle have moved upward to fill the empty space created by the diverging plates. The pressure on the mantle rocks decreases when they move upward, causing the mantle rocks to partially melt. This melting generates a large amount of basaltic magma that cools and crystallizes to form new oceanic crust between the diverging continents. Once the process of creating oceanic crust between the diverging plates starts, it becomes fairly stable, the plates may continue to diverge, and large ocean basins such as the Atlantic Ocean may form, with all of the rocks of the seafloor and oceanic crust forming since the plates diverged filling the gap between the continents as they move apart.

3

Transform Plate Boundaries and Transform Faults

A long the second type of plate boundary, tectonic plates slide past each other without the creation or the destruction of any significant amounts of new crust. These types of plate margins are known as transform boundaries, and are characterized by many strike-slip faults and earthquakes.

The mid-ocean ridges are apparently offset along great escarpments or faults in many places in the oceanic basins. These faults fragment the oceanic crust into many different segments. In 1965, the Canadian geophysicist J. Tuzo Wilson correctly interpreted these not as offsets, but as a new class of faults, known as transform faults. The actual sense of displacement on these faults is opposite to the apparent "offset" of the ridge segments, so the offset is not real but is an artifact of their original geometry. It is a primary feature of Wilson's model, proven correct by earthquake studies that are able to tell which direction the rocks on either side of the fault have moved.

These transform faults are steps in the plate boundary where one plate is sliding past the other plate. Transform faults are also found on some continents, with the most famous examples being the San Andreas Fault of California, the Dead Sea transform fault of the Middle East, the North Anatolian fault of Turkey, and the Alpine fault of New Zealand. All of these are large strike-slip faults with horizontal displacements, and all separate two different plates. Each of these faults penetrates the entire thickness of the lithosphere, and is connected to plate boundaries at both of their ends.

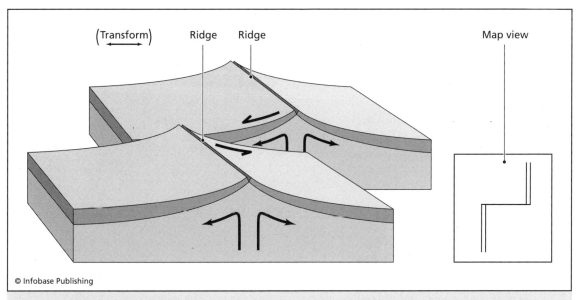

Three-dimensional view of a transform fault along the mid-ocean ridge, apparently offsetting a segment of the ridge. The sense of motion on the transform is opposite to the apparent offset. Note that the lateral motion between the two segments of the oceanic crust ceases once the opposite ridge segment is passed. At this point, magmas from the ridge intrude the transform, and the contact becomes igneous.

Transform Margin Processes

Processes that occur where two plates are sliding past each other along a transform plate boundary, either in the oceans or on the continents, are known as transform plate margin processes. Famous examples of transform plate boundaries on land include

- the San Andreas Fault in California
- the Dead Sea transform fault in the Middle East
- the East Anatolian transform fault in Turkey
- the Alpine fault in New Zealand
- the Altyn Tagh and Red River faults in Asia

Transform boundaries in the oceans are numerous, including the many transform faults that separate segments of the mid-ocean ridge system. Some of the larger transform faults in the oceans include the Romanche in the Atlantic, the Cayman fault zone on the northern edge of the Caribbean plate, and the Eltanin, Galápagos, Pioneer, and Mendocino fault zones in the Pacific Ocean.

There are three main types of transform faults, including

- those that connect segments of divergent boundaries (ridge-ridge transforms)
- offsets in convergent boundaries
- those that transform the motion between convergent and divergent boundaries

Satellite image of Dead Sea along the Dead Sea transform fault. Dead Sea transform fault is shown as a dashed line. The Dead Sea is the dark area (water) between the two strands of the fault. *(T. Kusky)*

Ridge-ridge transforms connect spreading centers and develop because in this way, they minimize the ridge segment lengths and minimize the dynamic resistance to spreading. Ideal transforms have purely strike-slip motions, and maintain a constant distance from the pole of rotation for the plate.

Transform segments in subduction boundaries are largely inherited configurations formed in an earlier tectonic regime. In collisional boundaries the inability of either plate to be subducted may lead to the formation of a long-lived zone of weakness that typically experiences strike-slip motions. Other transform faults may compensate the relative motion of minor plates in complex collisional zones, such as the Anatolian fault in Turkey that compensates for motions between Africa and Eurasia.

The development of a divergent-convergent boundary is best represented by the evolution of the San Andreas–Fairweather fault system. When North America overrode the East Pacific rise, the relative velocity between each plate was such that a transform fault formed to allow the sideways movement of the Pacific plate with respect to North America, with a migrating triple junction that lengthened the transform boundary.

Transform Boundaries in the Continents

Transform faults in continents show strike-slip offsets during earthquakes, and are high angle faults with dips greater than 70°. They never occur as a single fault, but rather as a set of subparallel faults. The faults are typically subparallel because they form along theoretical slip lines (along small circles about the pole of rotation), but the structural grain of the rocks interferes with this prediction. The differences between theoretical and actual fault orientations leads to the formation of segments that have pure strike-slip motions, and segments with contractional and extensional components of motion.

Extensional segments of transform boundaries form at left steps in left-slipping (left lateral) faults, and at right steps in right-slipping (right lateral) faults. Movement along fault segments with extensional bends generates gaps where deep basins known as pull-apart basins form. There are presently about 60 active pull-apart basins on the planet, including places like the Salton trough along the San Andreas Fault, and the Dead Sea along the Dead Sea transform fault. Pull-apart basins tend to form with an initially S-shaped or sigmoidal form, but as movements on the faults continue, the basins become very elongated parallel to the bounding faults. In some cases, the basin may extend so much that oceanic crust is generated in the center of the pull-apart, such as along the Cayman fault in the Caribbean. Pull-apart basins have stratigraphic and sedimentologic characteristics similar to rifts, including rapid lateral variations in the types of rocks deposited, such as basin-marginal fanglomerate and conglomerate deposits, interior lake basins, and local bimodal volcanic rocks. They are typically deformed soon after they form however, with folds and faults typical of strike-slip regime deformation.

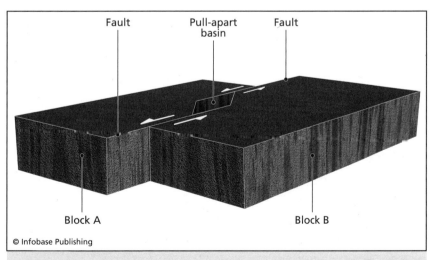

Block diagram of pull-apart basin. Continental crust in Block B has moved along the fault relative to Block A. A bend in the fault causes a space to open up during movement. This space becomes filled with sediments, and is known as a pull-apart basin.

Compressional bends form at bends in strike-slip fault systems where the shape of the bend causes the two blocks on opposites sides of the fault to be pressed into one another. Thus, steps to the right, known as right bends, in left lateral faults, and left steps in right lateral faults have contraction across the areas of the bend, even though the main part of the fault is simply sliding past the other side without contraction. These areas are characterized by mountain ranges and thrust faulted terrain that uplift and aid erosion of the extra volume of crust compressed into the bend in the fault. Examples of compressional (or restraining) bends include the Transverse Ranges along the San Andreas Fault, and Mount McKinley along the Denali Fault in Alaska. Many of the faults that form along compressional bends have low-angle dips at large distances from the main strike-slip fault, but progressively steeper dips toward the center of the main fault. This

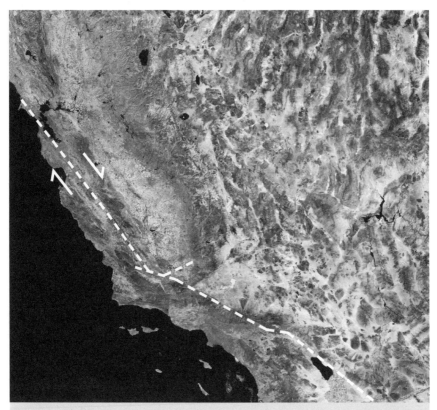

Satellite image of the Transverse Ranges along the San Andreas Fault in California. The trace of the San Andreas Fault is shown as the dashed line, with sense of movement indicated by arrows. *(T. Kusky)*

Satellite image of Mount McKinley along the Denali Fault in Alaska. The Denali Fault forms the linear valley that curves across the center of the image, and McKinley is the snow-covered peak south of the fault. *(T. Kusky)*

forms a distinctive geometry known as a flower or palm tree structure, with a vertical strike-slip fault in the center, and branches of mixed thrust/strike-slip faults branching off the main fault.

In a few places along compressional bends, two thrust-faulted mountain ranges may converge, forming a rapidly subsiding basin between the faults. These basins are known as ramp valleys. Many ramp valleys started as pull-apart basins, and became ramp valleys when the fault geometries changed.

A distinctive suite of structures that form in predictable orientations characterizes transform plate margins. Compressional bends form at high angles to the principal compressive stress, and at about 30–45° from the main strike-slip zone. These are often associated with *flower structures,* containing a strike-slip fault at depth, and folds and thrusts near the surface. Extensional or dilational bends often initiate with their long axes perpendicular to the compressional bends, but large amounts of extension may lead to the long axis being parallel to the main fault zone. Folds, often arranged in staircase-like, or stepped "en echelon" manner, typically form at about 45° from the main fault zone, with the fold axes developed perpendicular to the main compressive stress. The orientation with respect to the fault zone of many of these structures can be used to infer the sense of movement along the main transform faults.

Strike-slip faults along transform margins often develop from a series of en echelon fractures that initially develop in the rock. As the strain builds up, the fractures are cut by new sets of fractures known as Riedel fractures, in new orientations. Eventually, after several sets of oblique fractures have cut the rock, the main strike-slip fault finds the weakest part of the newly fractured rock through which to propagate, forming the main fault.

Transform Boundaries in the Oceans

Transform plate boundaries in the oceans include the system of ridge-ridge transform faults that are an integral part of the mid-ocean ridge system. Magma upwells along the ridge segments, cools, and crystallizes, becoming part of one of the diverging plates. The two plates then slide past each other along the transform fault between the two ridge segments, until the plate on one side of the transform meets the ridge on the other side of the transform. At this point, the transform fault is typically intruded by mid-ocean ridge magma, and the apparent extension of the transform, known as a fracture zone, juxtaposes two segments of the same plate that move together horizontally. Fracture zones are not extensions of the transform faults since they are no longer plate boundaries. After the ridge/transform intersection is passed, the fracture zone juxtaposes two segments of the same plate. There is typically some vertical motion along this segment of the fracture zone, since the two segments of the plate have different ages, and subside at different rates.

The transform and ridge segments remain at right angles in almost all cases, because this geometry creates a least work configuration, producing the shortest length of ridge possible on the spherical Earth. Transform faults generate very complex geological relationships. They juxtapose rocks from very different crustal and even mantle horizons, show complex structures, alteration by high-temperature metamorphism, and have numerous igneous intrusions. Rock types along oceanic transforms typically include suites of serpentinite, gabbro, pillow lavas, ultramafic peridotites (lherzolites and harzburgites), and even strongly metamorphosed oceanic crust rocks known as amphibolite-tectonites and mafic granulites.

Rocks preserved along transform faults record a very complex history of motion between the two oceanic plates. The relative motion includes dip-slip (vertical) motions due to subsidence related to the cooling of the oceanic crust. A component of dip-slip motion occurs all

TANYA ATWATER
(1942–)

The San Andreas Fault in California is one of the world's best-exposed continental transforms, and its history was largely unraveled by pioneering studies by the American tectonicist Tanya Atwater in the 1970s. Atwater is a professor of tectonics at the University of California at Santa Barbara. Her research has concerned various aspects of tectonics, ranging from sea floor spreading processes to global aspects of plate tectonics. She has participated in or led numerous oceanographic expeditions in the Pacific and Atlantic Oceans, including 12 dives to the deep seafloor in the tiny submersible, *Alvin*. She is especially well known for her works on the plate tectonic history of western North America, in general, and of the San Andreas Fault system. Her papers on the San Andreas Fault system led to widespread understanding of how the interactions of different subducting plates can lead to the formation of a continental transform fault from a plate margin that previously had convergent motions along it.

Atwater is devoted to science communication, teaching students at all levels in the university, presenting numerous workshops and field trips for K-12 teachers, consulting for the written media, museums, and television and video producers. Atwater serves on various national and international committees and panels. She is a fellow of the American Geophysical Union and the Geological Society of America and was a cowinner of the Newcomb Cleveland Prize of the American Association for the Advancement of Science and was elected to the prestigious National Academy of Sciences in 1997. She received her education at the Massachusetts Institute of Technology, the University of California at Berkeley, and Scripps Institute of Oceanography, completing her Ph.D. in 1972. She was a professor at the Massachusetts Institute of Technology before joining the faculty at U.C.S.B. in 1980.

along the transform, except at one critical point, known as the crossover point, where the transform juxtaposes oceanic lithosphere of the same age formed at the two different ridge segments. This dip-slip motion occurs along with the dominant strike-slip motion, recording the sliding of one plate past the other.

Fracture zones are also called the non-transform extension region. The motion along the fracture zone is purely dip-slip, due to the different ages of the crust with different subsidence rates on either side of the fracture zone. The amount of differential subsidence decreases with increasing distance from the ridge, and the amount of dip-slip motion decreases to near zero after about 60 million years. Subsidence decreases according to the square root of age, meaning that subsidence is initially rapid and slows with time.

Transform faults in the ocean may juxtapose crust with vastly different ages, thickness, temperature, and elevation. These contrasts often lead to the development of a deep topographic hole on the ridge axis at the intersection of the ridge and transform. The cooling effects of the older plate against the ridge of the opposing plate influences the axial rift topography all along the whole ridge segment, with the highest topographic point on the ridge being half way between two transform segments. Near transform zones, magma will be cooled before it reaches its normal level of hydrostatic equilibrium because of the cooling effects of the older cold plate adjacent to it. This cooling effect will change the types and amounts of magma erupted along the ridge near the transform, leading to different magma types along mid-ocean ridges.

The fault planes along transform faults are not typically vertical planes, nor are they always straight lines connecting two ridge segments. The fault planes typically curve toward the younger plate with depth, since they tend to seek the shortest distance through the lithosphere to the region of melt. This is a least energy configuration, and it is easier to slide a plate along a vertically short transform than along a thicker fault. This vertical curvature of the fault causes a slight change in the position and orientation of the fault on the surface, causing it to bend toward each ridge segment. These relationships cause the depth of earthquakes to decrease away from the crossover point, due to the different depth of transform fault penetration. Motion on these curved faults also influences the shape and depth of the transform-ridge intersection, enhancing the topographic depression and in many cases causing the ridge to curve slightly into the direction of the transform. Faults and igneous dikes also curve away from the strike of the ridge, toward the direction of the transform in the intersection regions.

Many of the features of ridge-transform intersections are observable in some ophiolite complexes (on-land fragments of ancient oceanic lithosphere), including the Arakapas transform in Troodos, Cyprus, and the Coastal Complex in the Bay of Islands ophiolite in Newfoundland.

Conclusion

Tectonic plates may slide past one another without producing or destroying any new plate material, along fault systems known as transform faults. These fault systems are common in the oceans where the oceanic ridge system shows apparent step-like offsets, with the ridge segments joined by transform faults. Transform faults also mark boundaries between some plates on the continents where the motion between the plates is parallel to the boundary. The most famous examples of transform boundaries in the continents include the San Andreas Fault of California, the Dead Sea fault of the Middle East, and the Alpine fault of New Zealand.

4

Convergent Margins

Oceanic crust and lithosphere are being destroyed by sinking back into the mantle at the deep ocean trenches in a process called subduction. As the oceanic slabs sink downward, they experience higher temperatures that cause water and other volatiles (light elements, like carbon dioxide) to be released, causing melts to be generated in the mantle wedge overlying the subducting slab. These melts then move upward to intrude the overlying plate, where the magma may become contaminated by melting through and incorporating minerals and elements from the overlying crust. Since subduction zones are long narrow zones where large plates are being forced back into the mantle, the melting produces a long line of volcanoes above the down-going plate. These volcanoes form a volcanic arc, either on a continent or over an oceanic plate, dependant on which type of crust the overlying plate is composed. The volcanic arcs are known as island arcs if they form a chain of islands developed on an oceanic plate, and as continental margin arcs if they develop on elevated continental crust.

Island arcs are extremely important for understanding the origin of the continental crust because the magmas and sediments produced in these systems have the same composition as the average continental crust. A simple model for the origin of the continental crust is that it represents a group of island arcs that formed at different times and then collided during plate collisions.

Since the plates are in constant motion, island arcs, continents, and other *terranes* often collide with each other. Mountain belts or orogens typically mark the places where lithospheric plates have collided, and the zone that they collided along is referred to as a suture. Suture zones are very complex, and include folded and faulted sequences of rocks that form on the two colliding terranes and in any intervening ocean basin. Often, slices of the old ocean floor are caught in these collision zones (geologists

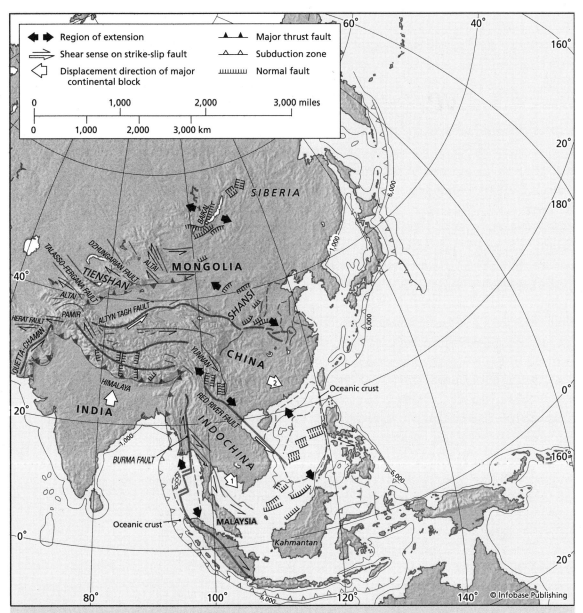

Map of central and eastern Asia showing the wide area affected by the collision of India with Asia

call these ophiolites), and the process by which they are emplaced over the continents is called obduction (opposite of subduction).

Subduction in some cases brings two continental plates together, which collide forming huge mountain belts like the Himalaya Mountain chain. In continent/continent collisions, deformation may be very diffuse and extend well beyond the normal limit of plate boundary deformation that characterizes other types of plate interactions. For example, the India-Asia collision has formed the huge uplifted Tibetan Plateau, and a series of mountain ranges to the north including the Tian Shan and Karakoram, and deformation of the continents extends far into Asia as far as Lake Baikal in Siberia.

Convergent Plate Margin Processes

Convergent plate margin processes include those geological processes that occur in the region affected by forces associated with the convergence of two or more plates. Convergent plate boundaries are of two fundamental types:

- subduction zones
- *collision zones*

Subduction zones are, in turn, of two basic types, the first being where oceanic lithosphere of one plate descends beneath another oceanic plate, such as in the Philippines and Marianas of the Southwest Pacific. The second type of subduction zone forms where an oceanic plate descends beneath a continental upper plate, such as in the Andes of South America. The southern Alaska convergent margin is particularly interesting, as it records a transition from an ocean/continent convergent boundary to an ocean/ocean convergent boundary in the Aleutians.

Southern Alaska's Convergent Margin

Southern Alaska is a convergent margin underlain by a complex collage of accreted terranes, including the Wrangellia superterrane and farther outboard, the Chugach–Prince William superterrane. During much of the Mesozoic, the two superterranes formed a magmatic arc and accretionary wedge, respectively, above a subduction zone that stretched around the edges of the Pacific Ocean. Southern Alaska is a beautiful region, but one prone to earthquakes, landslides, volcanic eruptions, and the whims of surging and calving (becoming detached) glaciers. The Border Ranges fault forms the boundary between the Wrangellia and Chugach–Prince

Satellite image of southern Alaska showing, from ocean toward the continental interior, the uplifted accretionary prism, Cook Inlet forearc basin, arc volcanoes (Mount Augustine, and Aleutian–Alaskan range), and continent. *(T. Kusky)*

William superterranes; it initiated as a subduction thrust but has been reactivated in various places as a strike-slip or normal fault. On the Kenai Peninsula the Chugach terrane contains two major units, the McHugh complex and the Valdez group. Farther inboard lies the McHugh complex, composed mainly of a complexly faulted and folded mixture of basalt, *chert,* argillite and graywacke, as well as several large ultramafic massifs that resemble pieces of oceanic crust. Fossil radiolarians from McHugh cherts throughout south-central Alaska range in age from Middle Triassic to mid-Cretaceous. The interval during which the McHugh complex formed by subduction and an offscraping process called *accretion* is not well known, but probably spanned most of the Jurassic and Cretaceous. The McHugh has been thrust seaward on the Eagle River–Chugach Bay fault over a relatively coherent tract of trench sediments known as *turbidites,* assigned to the Upper Cretaceous Valdez group. After the protracted episode of subduction-accretion that built the Chugach terrane, the accretionary wedge was cut by a series of granitic rocks that formed unusually close to the trench. These near-trench intrusive rocks, assigned to the Sanak-Baranof plutonic belt, are probably related to ridge subduction where a mid-ocean ridge system was pushed into the trench in one of the most unusual processes known in plate tectonics.

The McHugh complex of south-central Alaska and its lateral equivalent, the Uyak complex of Kodiak, are part of the Mesozoic/Cenozoic subduction complex of the Chugach terrane. Rocks similar to the McHugh in other circum-Pacific convergent margins include the Franciscan of California and the Shimanto of Japan. The evolution of the McHugh and its equivalents can be broken down into three broad, somewhat overlapping phases:

- origin of igneous and sedimentary protoliths;
- incorporation into the subduction complex ("accretion"), and attendant deformation and metamorphism; and
- younger deformations.

Fossil *radiaolarian* ages are readily explained by a stratigraphic model in which the McHugh basalts were formed by seafloor spreading, the overlying cherts were deposited on the ocean floor as it was conveyed toward a trench, and the argillite and graywacke record deposition in the trench, just prior to subduction and accretion. The timing of subduction and accretion is not well known, but probably spanned most of the Jurassic and Cretaceous. Limestone blocks in the McHugh complex might represent the tops of seamounts that were decapitated at the subduction zone.

The seaward part of the Chugach terrane is underlain by the Valdez group of late Cretaceous age. In the Kenai Peninsula, it includes medium- and thin-bedded graywacke turbidites, black argillite, and minor pebble to cobble conglomerate. These strata were probably deposited in a deep-sea trench and accreted shortly thereafter. Most of the Valdez group consists of relatively coherent strata, deformed into regional-scale folds, cut by a slaty cleavage. The McHugh complex and Valdez group are juxtaposed along a thrust, which in the area of Turnagain arm has been called the Eagle River fault, and on the Kenai Peninsula is known as the Chugach Bay *thrust*. Beneath this thrust is a complexly mixed rock known as *mélange*, consisting of partially to thoroughly disrupted Valdez group turbidites. Mélanges are mixtures of many different rock types typically including blocks of oceanic basement or limestone in muddy, shaly, serpentinitic, or even a cherty matrix. Mélanges are formed by tectonic mixing of the many different types of rocks found in the forearc, and are one of the hallmarks of convergent boundaries. This mélange is made only of blocks of graywacke mixed in a shaly matrix, which is quite distinct from the multi-component mélanges of the McHugh complex, can be traced for many kilometers in the footwall of the Eagle River thrust and its along-strike equivalents.

In early Tertiary time, near-trench intrusive rocks forming the Sanak–Baranof plutonic belt cut the Chugach accretionary wedge. The near-trench magmatic pulse migrated 1,367 miles (2,200 km) along the continental margin, from about 63–65 million years ago at Sanak Island in the west, to about 50 million years ago at Baranof Island in the east. These intrusive rocks are associated with many young brittle faults and gold-bearing quartz veins. The Paleogene near-trench magmatism was related to subduction of the Kula–Farallon spreading center.

(opposite page) Physiography and geology of arcs: (A) Pacific type; (B) Andean type

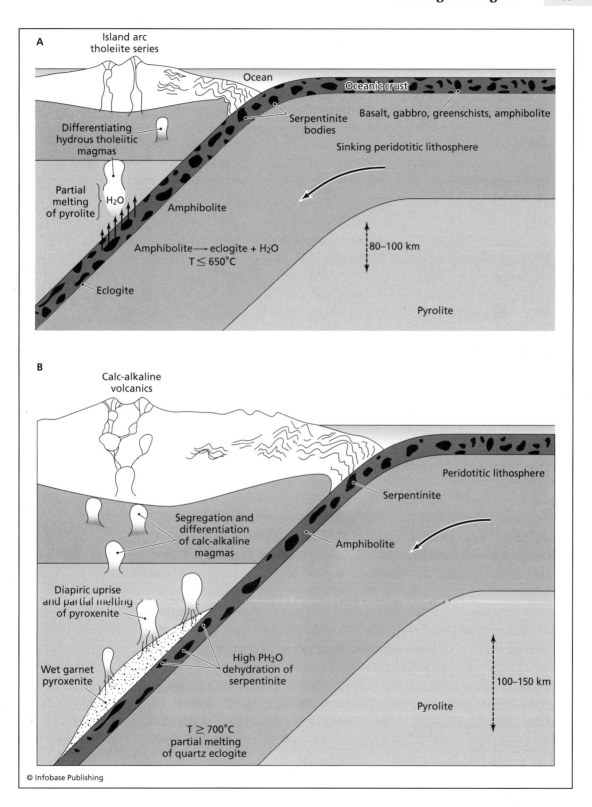

A

Island arc tholeiite series

Ocean

Oceanic crust

Basalt, gabbro, greenschists, amphibolite

Serpentinite bodies

Differentiating hydrous tholeiitic magmas

Sinking peridotitic lithosphere

Partial melting of pyrolite

H_2O

Amphibolite

Amphibolite $\longrightarrow$ eclogite + H_2O
$T \leq 650°C$

80–100 km

Eclogite

Pyrolite

B

Calc-alkaline volcanics

Peridotitic lithosphere

Serpentinite

Segregation and differentiation of calc-alkaline magmas

Amphibolite

Diapiric uprise and partial melting of pyroxenite

High PH_2O dehydration of serpentinite

Wet garnet pyroxenite

100–150 km

Pyrolite

$T \geq 700°C$ partial melting of quartz eclogite

Arcs

Most volcanic arcs are characterized by having several different topographic and geomorphic zones that are elongate parallel to the associated subduction zone that typically lies offshore in the ocean. The active arc is the topographically high zone with volcanoes, and the *backarc* region stretches from the active arc away from the trench, and it may end in an older rifted arc or continent. The arc is succeeded seaward by the *forearc* basin, a generally flat topographic basin with shallow to deep-water sediments, typically deposited over older accreted sediments and ophiolitic or continental basement. The accretionary prism includes uplifted strongly deformed rocks that were scraped off the downgoing oceanic plate on a series of faults that branch off from the subduction zone thrust fault. The trench may be five–seven miles (8–11 km) deep below the average level of the seafloor in the region and marks the boundary between the overriding and underthrusting plates. The outer trench slope is the region from the trench to the top of the flexed oceanic crust that forms a several hundred to one-thousand foot (few hundred-m) high topographic rise, known as the forebulge, on the downgoing plate.

Trench depressions are triangular shaped in profile and typically mostly filled with graywacke-shale sediments derived from erosion of the accretionary wedge, and deposited by sediment-laden, fast-moving down-slope flows known as turbidity currents. The resulting sedimentary rock types have a characteristic style of layering and an upward-decrease in grain size, and are known as turbidites. Turbidites may also be transported by currents along the trench axis for large distances, up to hundreds or even thousands of miles from their ultimate source in uplifted mountains in the convergent plate boundary orogen. *Flysch* is a term that applies to rapidly deposited deep marine syn-orogenic clastic rocks that are generally turbidites. Chaotic deposits known as olistostromes that typically have clasts or blocks of one rock type, such as limestone or sandstone, mixed with a muddy or shaly matrix also characterize trenches. These are interpreted as slump or giant submarine landslide deposits. They are common in trenches because of the oversteepening of slopes in the wedge. Sediments that get accreted may also include pelagic (deepwater) sediments that were initially deposited on the subducting plate, such as red clay, siliceous ooze, chert, manganiferous chert, calcareous ooze, and wind-blown dust.

The sediments are deposited as flat-lying turbidite packages, then gradually incorporated into the accretionary wedge complex through folding and the propagation of faults through the trench sediments. Subduction

Photograph of mélange in Alaska, showing blocks of rock within other rock types *(T. Kusky)*

accretion is a process that attaches sediments deposited on the underriding plate onto the base of the overriding plate. It causes the rotation and uplift of the *accretionary prism,* which is a broadly steady-state process that continues as long as sediment-laden trench deposits are thrust deeper into the trench. Typically, new faults will form and propagate beneath older ones, rotating the old faults and structures to steeper attitudes as new material is added to the toe and base of the accretionary wedge. This process increases the size of the overriding accretionary wedge and causes a progressive decrease in age of deformation toward the trench.

Parts of the oceanic basement to the subducting slab are sometimes scraped off and incorporated into the accretionary prisms. These tectonic slivers typically consist of fault-bounded slices of basalt, gabbro and ultramafic rocks, and rarely, partial or even complete ophiolite sequences can be recognized. These ophiolitic slivers are often parts of highly deformed belts of rock known as mélanges.

Variations between Different Types of Convergent Margin Arcs

There are major differences in processes that occur at continental or Andean-style versus oceanic or Marianas-style arc systems. Andean-type arcs have shallow trenches, less than four miles (6 km) deep, whereas Marianas-type arcs typically have deep trenches reaching seven miles (11 km) in depth. Most Andean-type arcs subduct young oceanic crust and have very shallow-dipping subduction zones, whereas Marianas-type arcs subduct old oceanic crust and have steeply dipping *Benioff zones*. Andean arcs have backarc regions dominated by foreland (retro-arc) fold thrust belts and sedimentary basins, whereas Marianas-type arcs typically have backarc basins, often with active seafloor spreading. Andean arcs have thick crust, up to 45 miles (70 km) thick, and big earthquakes in the overriding plate, while Marianas-type arcs have thin crust, typically only 12 miles (20 km) thick, and have big earthquakes in the underriding plate. Andean arcs have only rare volcanoes, and these have magmas rich in SiO_2 such as rhyolites and andesites. Plutonic rocks are more common, and the basement is continental crust. Marianas-type arcs have many volcanoes that erupt lava low in silica content, typically basalt, and are built on oceanic crust.

Many arcs are transitional between the Andean or continental margin types and the oceanic or Marianas types, and some arcs have large amounts of strike-slip motion. The causes of these variations have been investigated and it has been determined that the rate of convergence has little effect, but the relative motion directions and the age of the subducted oceanic crust seem to have the biggest effects. In particular, old oceanic crust tends to sink to the point where it has a near-vertical dip, rolling back through the viscous mantle, and dragging the arc and forearc regions of overlying Marianas-type arcs with it. This process contributes to the formation of backarc basins.

Much of the variation in the processes that occur in convergent margin arcs can be attributed to the relative convergence vectors between the overriding and underriding plates. In this *kinematic* approach to modeling convergent margin processes, the underriding plate may converge at any angle with the overriding plate, which itself moves toward or away from the trench. Since the active arc is a surface expression of the 70-mile (110-km) deep line on the subducted slab where most fluids are released, the arc will always stay 70 miles (110 km) above this zone. As the trench rolls back away from the arc, the arc therefore separates two parts on the overriding plate that may move independently, including the frontal arc sliver between the arc and trench, that is kinematically linked to the down-going plate, and the main part of the overriding plate. Different relative angles of convergence between the overriding and underriding plates determine whether or not an arc will have strike-slip motions, and the amount that the subducting slab rolls back (which is age dependent) determines whether the frontal arc sliver rifts from the arc and causes a backarc basin to open or not. This model helps to explain why some arcs are extensional with big backarc basins, others have strike-slip dominated systems, and others are purely compressional arcs. Convergent margins also show changes in these vectors and consequent geologic processes with time, often switching from one regime to the other quickly with changes in the parameters of the subducting plate.

As the cold subducting slab is pushed into the mantle it cools the surrounding mantle and forearc. Therefore, the effects of the downgoing

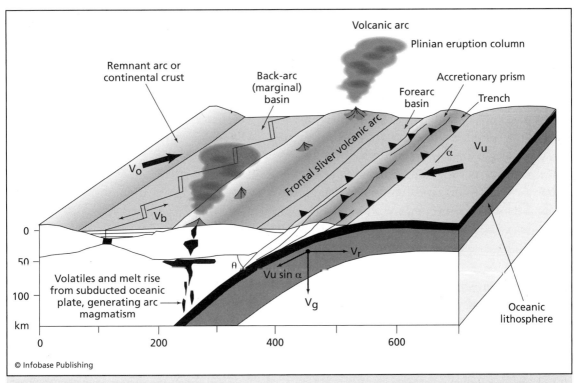

Relative motion vectors in arcs. Changes in relative motions can produce drastically different arc geology. V_u=velocity of underriding plate; V_o=velocity of overriding plate; V_b=slip vector between overriding and underriding plates; V_g=velocity of sinking; V_r=velocity of rollback. Note that V_u sin = velocity of downdip component of subduction, and $V_r =V_g$ cotθ.

slab dominate the thermal and fluid structure of arcs. Fluids released from the slab as it descends past 70 miles (110 km) aid partial melting in the overlying mantle and form the magmas that create the arc on the overriding plate. This broad thermal structure of arcs results in the formation of paired metamorphic belts, where the *metamorphism* in the trench environment grades from cold and low-pressure at the surface to cold and high-pressure at depth, whereas the arc records low and high-pressure high-temperature metamorphic *facies* series. One of the distinctive rock associations of trench environments is the formation of the unusual high-pressure low-temperature blueschist facies rocks in subduction zones. The presence of index minerals glaucophane (a sodic amphibole), jadeite (a sodic pyroxene), and lawsonite (Ca-zeolite) indicate low temperatures extended to depths of 20 miles (20–30 km). Since these minerals are unstable at high temperatures, their presence indicates they formed in a low temperature environment, and the cooling effects of the subducting plate offer the only known environment to maintain such cool temperatures at depth in the Earth.

Forearc basins may include several-kilometer thick accumulations of sediments that were deposited in response to subsidence induced by tectonic loading or thermal cooling of forearcs built on oceanic lithosphere. The Great Valley of California is a forearc basin that formed on oceanic forearc crust preserved in ophiolitic fragments found in central California, and Cook Inlet in Alaska is an active forearc basin formed in front of the Aleutian and Alaska range volcanic arc.

The rocks in the active arcs typically include several different facies. Volcanic rocks may include subaerial flows, tuffs, welded tuffs, volcaniclastic conglomerate, sandstone, and pelagic rocks. Debris flows from volcanic flanks are common, and there may be abundant and thick accumulations of ash deposited by winds and dropped by Plinian and other eruption columns. Volcanic rocks in arcs include mainly calc-alkaline series, showing early iron enrichment in the melt, typically including basalts, andesites, dacites, and rhyolites. Relatively young and undeveloped island arcs are strongly biased toward eruption on the mafic end of the spectrum, and may also include tholeiitic basalts, picrites (a magnesium rich basalt), and other volcanic and intrusive series. More mature continental arcs erupt more felsic rocks and may include large *caldera* complexes.

Backarc or marginal basins form behind extensional arcs, or may include pieces of oceanic crust that were trapped by the formation of a new arc on the edge of an oceanic plate. Many extensional back arcs

Satellite image of the Atacama Fault, Peruvian Andes. The fault is shown as the dashed white line.

are found in the southwest Pacific, whereas the Bering Sea between Alaska and Kamchatka is thought to be a piece of oceanic crust trapped during the formation of the Aleutian chain. Extensional backarc basins may have oceanic crust generated by seafloor spreading, and these systems very much resemble the spreading centers found at divergent plate boundaries. The geochemical signature of some of the lavas however show some subtle and some not-so-subtle differences, with water and volatiles being more important in the generation of magmas in backarc supra-subduction zone environments.

Compressional arcs such as the Andes have tall mountains, reaching heights of over 24,000 feet (7,315 m) over broad areas. They have rare or no volcanism but much plutonism, and typically have shallow dipping slabs beneath them. They have thick continental crust with large compressional earthquakes, and show a foreland-style retroarc basin in the backarc region. Some compressional arc segments do not have accretionary forearcs but exhibit subduction erosion during which material is eroded and scraped off the overriding plate, and dragged down into the subduction zone. The Andes show some remarkable along-strike variations in processes and tectonic style, with sharp boundaries between different segments. These variations seem to be related to what is being subducted and plate motion vectors. In areas where the downgoing slab has steep dips the overriding plate has volcanic rocks, in areas of shallow subduction there is no volcanism.

The Andes are a 5,000-mile (8,000-km) long mountain range in western South America, running generally parallel to the coast, between the Caribbean coast of Venezuela in the north and Tierra del Fuego in the south. The mountains merge with ranges in Central America and the West Indies in the north, and with ranges in the Falklands and Antarctica in the south. Many snow-covered peaks rise more than 22,000 feet (6,000 m), making the Andes the second tallest mountain belt in the world, after the Himalaya chain. The highest range in the Andes is the Aconcauga on the central and northern Argentine–Chile border. The high cold Atacama desert is located in the northern Chile sub-Andean range, and the high Altiplano Plateau is situated along the great bend in the Andes in Bolivia and Peru.

The southern part of South America consists of a series of different terranes added to the margin of the supercontinent Gondwana in the late Proterozoic and early Proterozoic. Subduction and the accretion of oceanic terranes continued through the Paleozoic, forming a 155-mile (250-km) wide accretionary wedge. The Andes formed as a continental margin volcanic arc system on the older accreted terranes, formed above a complex system of subducting plates from the Pacific Ocean. The uplift of the Andes is a relatively young geological event, having been raised mainly in the Cretaceous and Tertiary, with active volcanism and earthquakes. The specific nature of volcanism, plutonism, earthquakes, and uplift are found to be strongly segmented in the Andes, and related to the nature of the subducting part of the plate, including its dip and age. Regions above places where the subducting plate dips more than 30° have active volcanism, whereas regions above places where the subduction zone is sub-horizontal do not have active volcanoes.

The Altiplano is a large, uplifted plateau in the Bolivian and Peruvian Andes of South America. The plateau has an area of about 65,536 square miles (170,000 km²), and an average elevation of 12,000 feet (3,660 m) above sea level. The Altiplano is a sedimentary basin caught between the mountain ranges of the Cordillera Oriental on the east and the Cordillera Occidental on the west. Lake Titicaca, the largest high-altitude lake in the world, is located at the northern end of the Altiplano.

The Altiplano is a dry region with sparse vegetation, and scattered salt flats. Villagers grow potatoes and grains, and a variety of minerals are extracted from the plateau and surrounding mountain ranges.

Collisions

Collisions are the final products of subduction. There are several general varieties of collisions. They may be between island arcs and continents, such as modern Taiwan and China, or the Ordovician Taconic orogeny in eastern North America. Alternatively they may juxtapose passive margins on one continent and an Andean margin on another. More rarely, collisions between two convergent margins occur above two oppositely dipping subduction zones, with a contemporary example extant in the Molucca Sea of Indonesia. Finally, collisions may be between two continents, such as the ongoing India/Asia collision that is affecting much of Asia.

Collisions of island arcs with continents are the simplest of collisional events. As an arc approaches a continent, the continental margin is flexed downward by the weight of the arc, much like a ruler pushed down over the

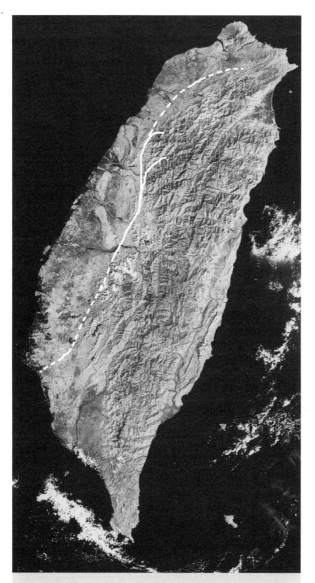

Satellite image of Taiwan, which is a sequence of deepwater sediments caught in the collision between the Luzon arc and Asia. The trace of the Cher-Lung-Pu fault is shown in white (solid white indicates the area that ruptured in the Chi-Chi earthquake of 1999). There are many other faults in Taiwan, and these form topographic lineaments visible on the image. *(T. Kusky)*

edge of a desk. The flexure induces a bulge a couple hundred miles (few hundred km) wide in front of the active collision zone, and this bulge migrates in front of the collision as a several hundred to thousand foot high (few hundred m) broad topographic high. As the arc terrane rides up onto the continent, the thick sediments in the continental rise are typically scraped off and progressively added to the accretionary prism, with the oldest thrust faults being the ones closest to the arc, and progressively younger thrust faults along the base of the prism. Many forearc regions have ophiolitic basement, and these ophiolites get thrust upon the continents during collision events and are preserved in many arc/continent collisional orogens. The accretionary wedge grows and begins to shed *olistostromes* into the foredeep basin between the arc and continent, along with flysch and distal black shales. These three main facies (belts of distinctive sediments deposited in a specific environment) migrate in front of the moving arc/accretionary complex at a rate equal to the convergence rate and drown any shallow water carbonate deposition. After the arc terrane rides up the continental rise, slope, and shelf, it grinds to a halt when isostatic (buoyancy) effects do not allow continued convergence. At this stage, a new subduction zone may be initiated behind the collided arc, allowing convergence to continue between the two plates.

Continent/continent collisions are the most dramatic of collisional events, with the current example of the convergence and collision of Africa, the Arabian Peninsula, and India with Europe and Asia, affecting much of the continental landmass of the world. Continental collisions are associated with thickening of continental crust and the formation of high mountains, and deformation distributed over wide areas. The convergence between India and Asia dramatically slowed about 38 million years ago, probably associated with initial stages of that collision The collision has resulted in the uplift of the Himalaya Mountain chain, the Tibetan plateau, and formed a wide zone of deformation that extends well into Siberia and includes much of Southeast Asia. Since the collision, there has been 2–2.4 inches per year (5–6 cm/yr) of convergence between India and Asia, meaning that a minimum of 775 miles (1,250 km) of shortening has had to be accommodated in the collision zone. This convergence has been accommodated in several ways. Two large faults between India and Asia—the Main Central thrust and the Main Boundary thrust—are estimated to have 250 mile (400 km) and 120 miles (200 km) of displacement on them, respectively, so they are able to account for less than half of the displacement. Folds of the crust and general shortening and thickening of the lithosphere may account for some of the convergence, but not a large amount. It appears that much

Satellite image of Tibet and the Himalaya Mountains, formed as a result of the collision of India and Asia. Note the sharp rise of the Himalaya Mountains out of the Indo-Gangetic plain (in the south), along a series of thrust faults. *(T. Kusky)*

THE TIBETAN PLATEAU

The Tibetan plateau is the largest high area of thickened continental crust on Earth, with an average height of 16,000 feet (4,880 m) over 470,000 square miles (1,220,000 km²). Bordered on the south by the Himalaya Mountains, the Kunlun Mountains in the north, the Karakorum on the west, and the Hengduan Shan on the east, Tibet is the source of many of the largest rivers in Asia. The Yangtze, Mekong, Salween, Indus, and Brahmaputra Rivers all rise in Tibet, and flow through Asia, forming the most important source of water and navigation for huge regions.

Southern Tibet merges into the foothills of the northern side of the main ranges of the Himalaya, but is separated from the mountains by the deeply incised river gorges of the Indus, Sutlej, and Yarlung Zangbo (Brahamaputra) Rivers. Central and northern Tibet consists of plains and steppes that are about 3,000 feet (1,000 m) higher in the south than the north. Eastern Tibet includes the Transverse Ranges (the Hengduan Shan) that are dissected by major faults in the river valleys of the northwest-southeast flowing Mekong, Salween, and Yangtze Rivers.

Tibet has a high plateau climate, with large diurnal and monthly temperature variations. The center of the plateau has an average January temperature of 32°F (0°C), and an average June temperature of 62°F (17°C). The southeastern part of the plateau is affected by the Bay of Bengal summer monsoons, whereas other parts of the plateau experience severe storms in fall and winter months.

Geologically, the Tibetan plateau is divided into four terranes, including the Himalayan terrane in the south, and the Lhasa terrane, the Qiangtang terrane, and Songban-Ganzi composite terrane in the north. The Songban-Ganzi terrane includes Triassic flysch and Carboniferous-Permian sedimentary rocks, and a peridotite-gabbro-diabase sill complex that may be an ophiolite, overlain by Triassic flysch. Another fault-bounded section includes Paleozoic limestone and marine clastics, probably deposited in an extensional basin. South of the Jinsha suture, the Qiangtang terrane contains Precambrian basement overlain by early Paleozoic sediments that are up to 12 miles (20 km) thick. Western parts of the Qiangtang terrane contain Gondwanan tillites, and Triassic-Jurassic coastal swamp and shallow marine sedimentary rocks. Late Jurassic–early Cretaceous deformation uplifted these rocks, before they were unconformably overlain by Cretaceous strata.

The Lhasa terrane collided with the Qiangtang terrane in the late Jurassic and formed the Bangong suture, containing flysch and ophiolitic slices that now separate the two terranes. It is a composite terrane containing various pieces that rifted from Gondwana in the late Permian. Southern parts of the Lhasa terrane contain abundant Upper Cretaceous to Paleocene granitic plutons and volcanics, as well as Paleozoic carbonates, and Triassic–Jurassic shallow marine deposits. The center of the Lhasa terrane is similar to the south but with fewer magmatic rocks, whereas the north contains Upper Cretaceous shallow marine rocks that onlap the Upper Jurassic–Cretaceous suture.

The Himalayan terrane collided with the Lhasa terrane in the middle Eocene forming the ophiolite-decorated Yarlung Zangbo suture. Precambrian metamorphic basement is thrust over Sinian through Tertiary strata including Lower Paleozoic carbonates and Devonian clastics, overlain unconformably by Permo-Carboniferous carbonates. The Himalayan terrane contains Lower Permian Gondwanan flora, and probably represents the northern passive margin of Mesozoic India, with carbonates and clastics in the south, thickening to an all clastic continental rise sequence in the north.

The Indian plate rifted from Gondwana and started its rapid (3.2–3.5 inches per year; 8–9 cm/yr) northward movement about 120 million years ago. Subduction of the Indian plate beneath Eurasia

(continues)

(continued)

until about 70 million years ago formed the Cretaceous Kangdese batholith belt, containing diorite, granodiorite, and granite. Collision of India with Eurasia at 50–30 million years ago formed the Lhagoi-Khangari of biotite and alkali granite, and the 20–10 million-year old Himalayan belt of tourmaline-muscovite granites.

Tertiary faulting in Tibet is accompanied by volcanism, and the plateau is presently undergoing east-west extension with the formation of north-south graben associated with hot springs, and probably deep magmatism. Geophysical measurements have detected some regions with unusual characteristics beneath some of these graben, interpreted by some geologists as regions of melt or partially molten crust.

of the convergence was accommodated by underthrusting of the Indian plate beneath Tibet, and by strike-slip faulting moving or extruding parts of Asia out of the collision zone toward the southwest Pacific.

The Tibetan plateau and Himalaya Mountain chain are about 375 miles (600 km) wide, with the crust beneath the region being about 45 miles (70 km) thick, twice that of normal continental crust. This has led to years of scientific investigation about the mechanism of thickening. Some models and data suggest that India is thrust under Asia for 370 miles (600 km), whereas other models and data suggest that the region has thickened by thrusting at the edges and *plane strain* in the center. In either case, the base of the Tibetan crust has been heated to the extent that partial melts are beginning to form, and high heat flow in some rifts on the plateau is associated with the intrusions at depth. The intrusions are weakening the base of the crust, which is starting to collapse under the weight of the overlying mountains, and the entire plateau is on the verge of undergoing extension.

Geologists, geophysicists, and atmospheric scientists are currently focusing great amounts of research efforts toward understanding the timing of the uplift of the Tibetan plateau and modeling the role this uplift has had on global climate. The plateau strongly affects atmospheric circulation, and many models suggest that the uplift may contribute to global cooling and the growth of large continental ice sheets in late Tertiary and Quaternary times. In addition to immediate changes to air flow patterns around the high plateau, the uplift of large amounts of carbonate platform and silicate rocks are exposed to erosion. The weathering of these rocks causes them to react with atmospheric carbon dioxide, which combines these ions to produce bicarbonate ions such as $CaCO_3$, drawing down the atmospheric carbon dioxide levels and contributing to global cooling.

The best estimates of the time of initial collision between India and Asia is between 54 and 49 million years ago. Since then, convergence between India and Asia has continued, but at a slower rate of 1.6–2.0 inches per year (4–5 cm/yr), and this convergence has resulted in intense folding, thrusting, shortening, and uplift of the Tibetan plateau. Timing the uplift to specific altitudes is difficult, and considerable debate has centered on how much younger than 50 million years ago the plateau reached its current height of 16,404 feet (5 km). Most geologists would now agree that this height was attained by 13.5 million years ago, and that any additional height increase is unlikely since the strength of the rocks at depth has been exceeded, and the currently active east-west extensional faults are accommodating any additional height increase by allowing to crust to flow laterally.

When the plateau reached significant heights it began to deflect regional airflow currents that in turn deflect the jet streams, causing them to meander and change course. Global weather patterns were significantly changed. The cold polar jet stream is in particular now at times deflected southward over North America, Northwest Europe, and other places where ice sheets have developed. The uplift increased aridity in central Asia by blocking moist airflow across the plateau, leading to higher summer and cooler winter temperatures. The uplift also intensified the Indian Ocean monsoons, because the height of the plateau intensifies temperature-driven atmospheric flow as higher and lower pressure systems develop over the plateau during winter and summer. This has increased the amount of rainfall along the front of the Himalaya Mountains, where some of the world's heaviest rainfalls have been reported, as the Indian monsoons are forced over the high plateau. The cooler temperatures on the plateau led to the growth of glaciers, which in turn reflect back more sunlight, further adding to the cooling effect.

Studies of ancient climate records show that the Indian Ocean monsoon underwent strong intensification 7–8 million years ago, in agreement with some estimates of the time of uplift, but younger than other estimates. The effects of the uplift would be different if the uplift occurred rapidly in the late Pliocene–Pleistocene (as suggested by analysis of geomorphology, ancient cave sequences, and mammal fauna), or if the uplift occurred gradually since the Eocene (based on lake sediment analysis). Most geologists accept analysis of data that suggests that uplift began about 25 million years ago, with the plateau reaching its

Satellite image of egg-carton shaped folds in Madagascar, formed at deep levels in the crust during a continental collision 570 million years ago that formed the supercontinent of Gondwana *(T. Kusky)*

current height by 14 or 15 million years ago. These estimates are based on the timing of the start of extensional deformation that accommodated the exceptional height of the plateau, sedimentological records, and on uplift histories based on the records of temperatures preserved in some minerals.

The collisional process is resulting in the formation of a layered differentiated lower continental crust in Tibet with granitic melts forming a layer that has been extracted from a *granulitic* residue, along with strong deformation. These processes are not readily observable 30 miles (50 km) beneath Tibet, but are preserved in many very old (generally Precambrian) high-grade gneiss terranes around the world that are thought to have formed in continental collision zones.

Continent/continent collision zones tend to have major effects on global plate motions. Convergence that used to be accommodated between the two continents must be transferred elsewhere on the planet, since all plate motions must sum to zero on the planet. Therefore, continental collisions typically cause events elsewhere, such as the formation of new subduction zones and a global reorganization of plate motions.

Most areas within the continents experience little deformation and suffer few earthquakes since they are located far from plate boundaries. An exception is the broad area of intracontinental deformation associated with the India–Asia collision described above. Most geologists regard this area as an exceptionally wide plate boundary zone or an area characterized by many small microplates that are all moving and deforming relative to one another.

Most continental interiors are characterized by broad areas of flat lying sedimentary rocks overlying Precambrian basement. These areas are known as platforms. In contrast, where the Precambrian basement is exposed over a broad area, the region is called a shield. In areas that have recently been deglaciated such as Canada and Scandanavia, many shields and platforms are experiencing a slow broad uplift (up to a tenth of an inch, or several mm per year). This is a response to the removal of the weight of the glaciers, and is known as glacial rebound.

In many places in the continents Precambrian basement rocks are exposed in small isolated uplifts, or hilly country. Examples in North America include the Adirondack Mountains in New York, the Llano uplift in Texas, and the Black Hills and Sioux uplift of South Dakota. Contrasting with the uplifts, other parts of continental interiors are characterized by abnormal subsidence forming deep interior basins. Examples include the three mile (4 km) deep Michigan and Illinois basins of the central United States. These basins are thought to have formed by a combination of forces from collisions on the plate edges, and from a cooling and thermal subsidence above older, previously heated rift basins. When the rocks at depth cool, they become denser and sink, causing the surface to sink as well, forming basins.

Conclusion

Convergent margins represent the boundary between two tectonic plates where two plates are moving toward each other. These margins have several fundamentally different types, including

- where two oceanic plates are moving toward each other, and one sinks below the other
- where an oceanic plate is moving toward and sinks under a continent
- where two continents are moving toward each other, uplifting great mountain ranges between them

Lines of volcanoes form above convergent margins where an oceanic plate is subducted beneath another plate, including island arcs where two ocean plates converge, and continental margin arcs where a continent is moving over an oceanic plate. All convergent margins can change into collisional margins when continental or arc material on one plate moves into contact with continental crust of the opposing plate. Since continents are relatively light and buoyant compared to the mantle, they crumble and deform when they collide with another continent, forming some of the tallest mountain chains in the world, such as the Himalaya Mountains where India is crashing into Asia. Convergent margins are known to have the largest and most destructive earthquakes out of all the types of plate boundaries.

Part II

■ ■ ■

Earthquakes

5

Earthquakes

An *earthquake* occurs when a sudden release of energy causes the ground to shake and vibrate, associated with passage of waves of energy released at its source. Earthquakes can be extremely devastating and costly events, sometimes killing tens or even hundreds of thousands of people and leveling entire cities in a matter of a few seconds or minutes. Recent earthquakes have been covered in detail by the news media and the destruction and trauma of those affected is immediately apparent. A single earthquake may release the energy equivalent to hundreds or thousands of nuclear blasts, and may cost billions of dollars in damage, not to mention the toll in human suffering. Earthquakes are also associated with secondary hazards, such as *tsunamis*, landslides, fire, famine, and disease that also exert their toll on humans. The causes and consequences of earthquakes are examined in detail in this chapter. This provides a context for a discussion of where earthquakes are most likely to occur, how they are studied, plus the hazards associated with earthquakes, their cost, and what might be done to reduce their devastating effects.

As described in the last several chapters, the lithosphere (or outer rigid shell) of the Earth is broken into about twelve large tectonic plates, each moving relative to the other. There are many other smaller plates. Most of the earthquakes in the world happen where two of these plates meet and are moving past each other, such as in southern California. Recent earthquakes in Turkey, Taiwan, Sumatra, Mexico, and Pakistan have also been located along plate boundaries. A map on page 16 of plate boundaries of the Earth and earthquakes shows where significant earthquakes have occurred in the past 50 years. Most large earthquakes occur at boundaries where the plates are moving toward each other (as in Alaska and Japan), or sliding past one another (as in southern California and Turkey). Smaller earthquakes occur where the plates are moving apart, such as along mid-oceanic ridges where new magma rises and forms oceanic spreading centers.

In the conterminous (the lower 48) United States the area that suffers the most earthquakes is southern California along the San Andreas Fault, where the Pacific plate is sliding north relative to the North American plate. The motion in this area is characterized as a "stick-slip" type of sliding, where the two plates stick to each other along the plate boundary as the two plates slowly move past each other, bending the rocks and causing stresses to rise over tens or hundreds of years. Eventually the stresses along the boundary rise so high that the strength of the rocks is exceeded, and the rocks suddenly break, causing the two plates to dramatically move (slip) up to a few meters in a few seconds. This sudden motion of previously stuck segments along a fault plane is an earthquake. The severity of the earthquake is determined by how large of an area breaks in the earthquake, how far it moves, how deep

Photo of railroad tracks bent and displaced during earthquake, California *(USGS)*

within the Earth the break occurs, and the length of time that the broken or slipped area along the fault takes to move. The *elastic rebound theory* states that recoverable (also known as elastic) strains build up in a material until a specific level or breaking point is reached. When the breaking point or level is attained, the material suddenly breaks, releasing energy and stresses in an earthquake. In the case of earthquakes, rows of fruit trees, fences, roads, and railroad lines that became gradually bent across an active fault line as the stresses built up are noticeably offset across faults that have experienced an earthquake. When the earthquake occurs, the rocks snap along the fault, and the bent rows of trees, fences, or roads/rail-line become straight again, but displaced across the fault.

Areas at Risk for Significant Earthquakes in the United States

Some areas in the United States have a greater risk of experiencing earthquakes than other areas. The areas of greatest risk are mostly located in the western half of the country, where the Pacific and several smaller plates are interacting with the North American plate, often resulting in earthquakes. Earthquakes are rare but do occur in a few other places, such as St. Louis, Boston, and Charleston, South Carolina.

Within these areas of the western United States that are prone to earthquakes, several have an especially high risk because they are cut by segments of faults such as the San Andreas that are locked and have been building up strain for many years, and appear ready to break. Parts of the southern section of the San Andreas Fault in California fall into this category. Other areas such as Seattle may rest on gently dipping thrust faults that could release large amounts of seismic energy, causing destruction by ground shaking and tsunamis. In contrast, other areas such as parts of Alaska are prone to large earthquakes, but have a very low population density so pose a lower overall risk for damage and loss of life.

SOUTHERN CALIFORNIA

For many years there has been much speculation and analysis by the United States Geological Survey and other groups about the effects of the anticipated "big one," a possible > magnitude 8 earthquake that could strike southern California. This speculation and fear is not unfounded. The unrepentant forces of plate tectonics continue to slide the Pacific plate northward relative to North America along the San Andreas Fault, and the stick-slip type of behavior that characterizes segments of this fault system generates many earthquakes. Several segments of the fault have seismic gaps, where the tectonic stresses may be particularly built up. One of these gaps released its stress during the Loma Prieta earthquake of 1989, but other gaps remain, including the large area generally east of Los Angeles. Some models predict that the seismic energy may be released in this area by a series of moderate earthquakes (magnitude 7), but other, more sinister predictions also remain plausible. The last major rupture along the southern California segment was in 1857, and studies of prehistoric earthquakes in this region show that major, catastrophic events recur roughly every 140 years. In this scenario, the next major event has been expected sometime since the year 1997, with a large margin of error.

THE PACIFIC NORTHWEST

Until the mid-1980s, most people in the Seattle area thought they were far enough away from active faults to not worry about earthquakes. Scientists thought the Cascadia subduction zone beneath the Pacific Northwest was not the type to generate earthquakes, since it had not produced any earthquakes in a long time. Then, on February 28, 2001, a magnitude 6.8 earthquake lasting 45 seconds and injuring 250 people changed the way geologists thought about the Cascadia subduction zone. Since then, scientists and residents have come to realize that this subduction-type convergent margin forms a potential threat for earthquakes, even for great earthquakes (magnitude > 8) similar in magnitude to the December 26, 2004, Indonesian earthquake. In addition to the active seismicity, this realization comes in part from studies that have identified paleo-earthquakes and tsunami deposits from local earthquakes.

The United States Geological Survey has identified three main potential sources for Pacific Northwest earthquakes, including deep ruptures that originate along the subduction zone thrust, and have in the past generated magnitude 6.5–7.1 earthquakes in this area. The second potential source is within the upper plate over the subduction zone, where events greater than magnitude 7 have occurred in the past (1872, 1918, and 1946). The third source is potentially the most destructive, including the shallow segment of the subduction zone where ruptures can be large and include significant surface movements, generating tsunami. The most recent giant (~magnitude 9) shallow subduction zone quake here was in 1700, where the earthquake triggered a huge tsunami

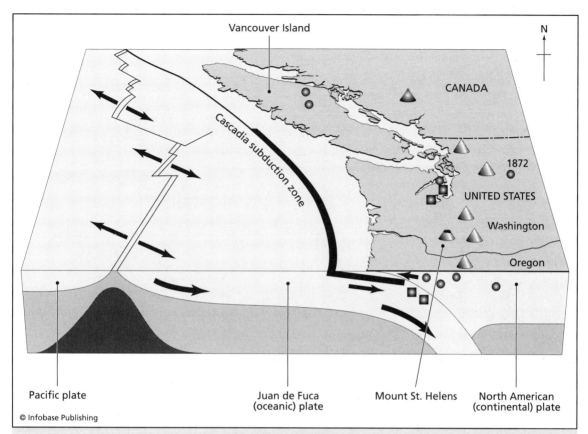

Pacific plate

Juan de Fuca
(oceanic) plate

Mount St. Helens

North American
(continental) plate

© Infobase Publishing

Three-dimensional block diagram of the Cascadia subduction zone showing different potential sources of earthquakes, including 1) the overriding plate, 2) the deep Benioff zone, and 3) the shallow trench, potentially generating a great earthquake and large tsunamis. Squares show locations of deep earthquakes (more than 30 miles [48 km]) and circles show locations of shallow earthquakes (less than 15 miles [24 km]). Triangles show locations of active volcanoes, the thick line along the Cascadia subduction zone shows the segment of this fault that ruptured in 1700, and circle shows location of 1872 earthquake. *(Modeled after diagram from the USGS)*

that damaged parts of Japan, and left deposits around the Pacific Northwest area. It is estimated that events of this size occur every 400–600 years in the Cascadia subduction zone, and the clock is ticking.

A magnitude 9 earthquake in the Cascadia subduction zone would be devastating to the Seattle–Tacoma–Aberdeen–Bellingham area, including at least several minutes of shaking (the Sumatra earthquake had up to 10 minutes of shaking), with peak ground accelerations exceeding half the force of gravity. Like San Francisco's infamous Nimitz Freeway that collapsed in the 1989 Loma Prieta earthquake, Seattle has double-decker freeways built on tidal flat deposits and uncompacted landfill deposits that are prone to severe shaking and liquefaction during earthquakes, potentially leading to highway collapse. Faults have recently been discovered running through downtown Seattle, suggesting that the region may be susceptible to strong earthquakes. The Seattle fault runs through Puget Sound then close to the Kingdome in downtown, and appears to have accommodated about 20 feet (6 m) of movement of a block measuring 10 miles (16 km) long by four miles (6.4 km) wide about 1,000 years ago. Shallow faults like this one have the potential to generate devastating earthquakes since their energy is released near the surface generating large amounts of ground shaking. Other geologic and natural features in the Seattle area all indicate that a major earthquake occurred here, such as landslide scars that mar many hillsides, some of which dammed valleys and formed lakes. Forests now observed on the bottoms of lakes died between 800 and 1,400 years ago perhaps from drowning associated with earthquake-induced changes in ground level. Sand deposits from tsunamis that inundated bayhead marshes have been tentatively correlated with a sudden uplift of parts of Puget Sound by more than 20 feet sometime between 500 and 1,700 years ago during a catastrophic earthquake, and other areas record sudden subsidence of about five feet (1.5 m) at 1,000 years ago.

Even more devastating would be an earthquake along the Cascadia subduction zone, with potential magnitudes exceeding 9. Besides the tremendous ground shaking, huge tsunamis could be generated, that would quickly sweep along the coastline. Sand layers in coastal swamps attest to a succession of tsunamis in the region, as recently as 300 years ago, though research is only beginning on these to understand their frequency and whether they were generated from local or distant earthquakes. Some coastal forests with Sitka spruce are dead, having been killed 300 years ago when the land dropped six to eight feet (1.8–2.4 m) putting the roots of the trees into salt water, killing them. The potential for great (magnitude > 9) earthquakes in the Cascadia subduction zone is clear, but the cities of Seattle, Portland, and regions in Washington, British Columbia, Oregon and northern California are not adequately prepared. Building codes are not as strict as in earthquake-prone southern California, yet the potential for exceptionally large earthquakes is greater in the Pacific Northwest.

Some areas away from active plate boundaries are also occasionally prone to earthquakes. Even though earthquakes in these areas are uncommon, they can be very destructive. Places including Boston, Massachusetts, Charleston, South Carolina, and New Madrid, Missouri (near St. Louis), have been sites of particularly bad earthquakes. In 1811 and 1812 three large earthquakes with magnitudes of 7.3, 7.5, and 7.8 were centered in New Madrid and shook nearly the entire United States causing widespread destruction. Most buildings were toppled near the origin of the earthquake, and several deaths were reported (the region only had a population of 1,000 at the time, but is now densely populated). Damage to buildings was reported from as far away as Boston and Canada, where chimneys toppled, plaster cracked, and church bells were set to ringing by the shaking of the ground.

Many earthquakes in the past have been incredibly destructive, killing hundreds of thousands of people, like the ones in Armenia, Iran, Mexico City, and Pakistan in recent years (see table below). Some earthquakes have killed nearly a million people, such as one in 1556 in China that killed 800,000–900,000 people, another in China in 1976 that killed an estimated 242,000 to 800,000 people, one in Calcutta, India in 1737

The 12 Deadliest Earthquakes in Recorded History

PLACE	YEAR	DEATHS	ESTIMATED RICHTER MAGNITUDE
Shaanxi, China	1556	830,000	
Calcutta, India	1737	300,000	
Sumatra, Indonesia	2004	283,000	9.0
T'ang Shan, China	1976	242,000 (could be as high as 800,000)	7.8
Gansu, China	1920	180,000	8.6
Messina, Italy	1908	160,000	7.5
Tokyo, Japan	1923	143,000	8.3
Beijing, China	1731	100,000	
Chihli, China	1290	100,000	
Naples, Italy	1693	93,000	
Muzaffarabad, Pakistan	2005	86,000	7.6
Gansu, China	1932	70,000	7.6

that killed about 300,000 people, and the earthquake-related Indian Ocean tsunami that killed an estimated 283,000 people in 2004.

Origins of Earthquakes

Earthquakes can originate from sudden motion along a fault, or from a volcanic eruption, bomb blasts, landslides, or anything that suddenly releases energy on or in the Earth. Not every fault is associated with active earthquakes. Most faults are in fact no longer active, but were active at some time in the geologic past. Of the faults that are active, only some are characterized as being particularly prone to earthquakes. Some faults are slippery, and the two blocks on either side just slide by each other passively without producing major earthquakes. In other cases, however, the blocks stick to each other and deform like a rubber band until they reach a certain point where they suddenly snap, releasing energy in an earthquake event.

Rocks and materials exhibit brittle behavior when they respond to built up tectonic pressures by cracking, breaking or fracturing. Earthquakes represent a sudden breaking of the rocks at depth as a brittle response to built-up stress, and are almost universally activated in the upper couple miles (few kilometers) of the Earth's crust. Deeper than this, the pressure and temperature are so high that the rocks simply deform like Silly Putty and do not snap, but flow in a ductile manner.

An earthquake originates in one place and then spreads out in all directions along the fault plane. The *focus* is the point in the Earth where the earthquake energy is first released and represents the area on one side of a fault that actually moves relative to the rocks on the other side of the fault plane. After the first slip event the area surrounding the focus experiences many smaller earthquakes as the surrounding rocks also slip past each other to even out the deformation caused by the initial earthquake shock. The *epicenter* is the point on the Earth's surface that lies vertically above the focus.

When big earthquakes occur, the surface of the Earth actually forms into waves that move across the surface, just as in the ocean. These waves can be pretty spectacular and also extremely destructive. When an earthquake strikes, these seismic waves move out in all directions, just like sound waves, or ripples that move across the water after a stone is thrown in a still pond. After the seismic waves have passed through the ground, the ground returns to its original shape, although buildings and other human constructions are commonly destroyed. Some people who have experienced really large earthquakes have actually seen waves of rock, several feet high, moving toward them at very high speeds.

During an earthquake, several types of seismic waves can either radiate underground from the focus—called *body waves*—or aboveground from the epicenter: *surface waves.* The body waves travel through the whole body of the Earth and move faster than surface waves, whereas surface waves cause most of the destruction associated with earthquakes

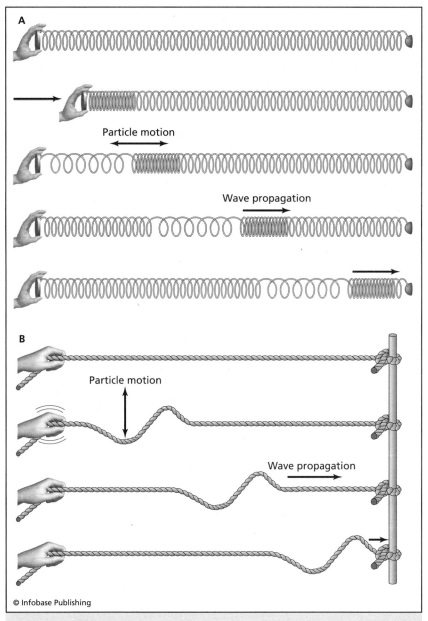

© Infobase Publishing

Analogy to seismic waves using slinky and ropes

because they briefly change the shape of the surface of the Earth when they pass. There are two types of body waves—P (Primary) or compressional waves and S waves, for shear or secondary waves. P waves deform material through a change in volume and density, and these can pass through solids, liquids and gases. The kind of movement associated with passage of a P wave is a back and forth type of motion. P waves move with high velocity, about 3.5–4 miles per second (6 km/sec), and are thus the first to be recorded by seismographs. This is why they are called primary

METHOD OF LOCATING EPICENTERS USING THREE INTERSECTING CIRCLES

It is very difficult to tell where the source or epicenter of an earthquake was located when the seismic waves pass through a different location. All the observer feels is a series of different waves that shake and move the surface in different ways, typically with a little time of quiet between the passage of each different type of wave. Seismologists are able to use some basic properties of the physics of seismic waves to determine where the epicenter of an earthquake is located soon after any event. Because both P and S waves have known rates of travel through the Earth, these different waves will arrive at the observer at different times. The P wave is fastest, traveling at 3.5–4 miles per second (6 km/sec), and are followed by the arrival of the S waves, that travel about half as fast, at two miles (3.5 km) per second. Seismologist record the type of motion made by the passage of each seismic wave as it passes, and pick which waves are the first P waves, and which are the first S waves. Then, the exact time of the arrival of the first P and first S waves is noted, and the difference between their arrival time is measured. This time difference is directly related to the distance from the epicenter—the further the distance, the greater the time difference between the arrival of the first P and the first S waves. If the time difference between the P and the S waves is two seconds, then we know that we are two miles from the epicenter (four miles per second minus two miles per second). If the time difference is 20 seconds, then we are 20 miles from the epicenter, and so on. Once the distance to the earthquake epicenter is known, this distance can be drawn as a circle around the observation point, and the seismologist knows that the earthquake epicenter is located somewhere on this circle.

To complete the calculation of where the earthquake epicenter is located, the seismologist needs more information from other locations. If there is information from one other location, then two circles showing the distance to the epicenter from two different points can be drawn, and these two circles will intersect in two places, giving two possible locations for the epicenter location. Therefore three observation points are needed to uniquely determine the epicenter location. Three circles should only intersect in one location, showing the location of the epicenter.

A final calculation is made; strength and height of the seismic waves would be at a distance of 60 miles (100 km) from the epicenter. This measurement is more complex, involving many variables such as the type of material the waves passed through, but is needed to assign a Richter magnitude to the earthquake. It often takes a longer time to make the second calculation of the Richter magnitude, and

(P) waves. P waves cause a lot of damage because they temporarily change the area and volume of ground that humans have built things on or modified in ways that require the ground to keep its original shape, area, and volume. When the ground suddenly changes its volume by expanding and contracting, many of these constructions break. For instance, if a gas pipeline is buried in the ground, it may rupture and explode when a P wave passes because of its inability to change its shape along with the Earth. It is common for fires and explosions originating from broken

this is why the estimated strength of an earthquake is often disputed or reported to be different by different groups immediately after an earthquake event.

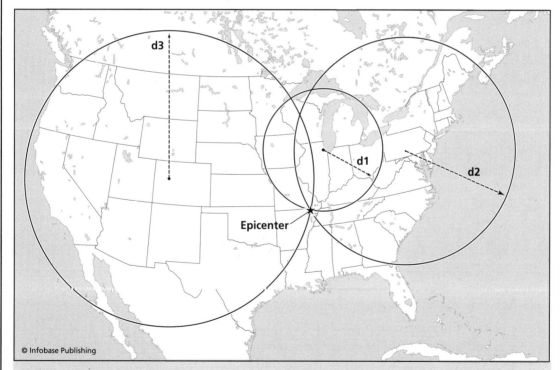

© Infobase Publishing

Method of locating earthquake epicenters, by calculating the distance to the source from three different seismic stations. The distance to the epicenter is calculated using the time difference between the first arrivals of P and S waves. The unique place that the three distance circles intersect is the location of the epicenter.

pipelines to accompany earthquakes. History has shown that fires often do as much damage after the earthquake as the ground shaking did during the earthquake. This fact is dramatically illustrated by the 1906 earthquake in San Francisco, where much of the city burned for days after the shaking, resulting in destruction of the city.

The second kind of body waves are known as *shear waves* (S) or secondary waves because they change the shape of a material but not its volume. Only solids can transmit shear waves, whereas liquids can not. Shear waves move material at right angles to the direction of wave travel and thus they consist of an alternating series of sideways motions. Holding a jump rope at one end on the ground, and moving it rapidly back and forth can simulate this kind of motion. Waves form at the end being held, and move the rope sideways as they move toward the loose end of the rope. A typical shear wave velocity is two miles per second (3.5 km/sec). These kinds of waves may be responsible for knocking buildings off foundations when they pass, since their rapid sideways or back and forth motion is often not met by buildings. The effect is much like pulling a tablecloth out from under a set table—if done rapidly, the building (as is the case for the table setting) may be left relatively intact, but detached from its foundation.

Surface waves can also be extremely destructive during an earthquake. These have complicated types of twisting and circular motions, much like the circular motions exhibited by waves out past the surf zone at the beach. Surface waves travel slower than either type of body waves, but because of their complicated types of motion they often cause the most damage. This is a good thing to remember during an earthquake, because if the body waves have just passed a specific location, there may be a brief period of no shaking to allow residents of the area to escape outside before the very destructive surface waves hit and cause even more destruction.

Measuring Earthquakes

How is the shaking of an earthquake measured? Geologists use seismographs, which display earth movements by means of an ink-filled stylus on a continuously turning roll of graph paper. Modern seismographs have digital versions of the same design, but record the data directly to computer systems for analysis. When the ground shakes, the needle wiggles and leaves a characteristic zigzag line on the paper. Many seismograph records clearly show the arrival of P and S body waves, followed by the surface waves.

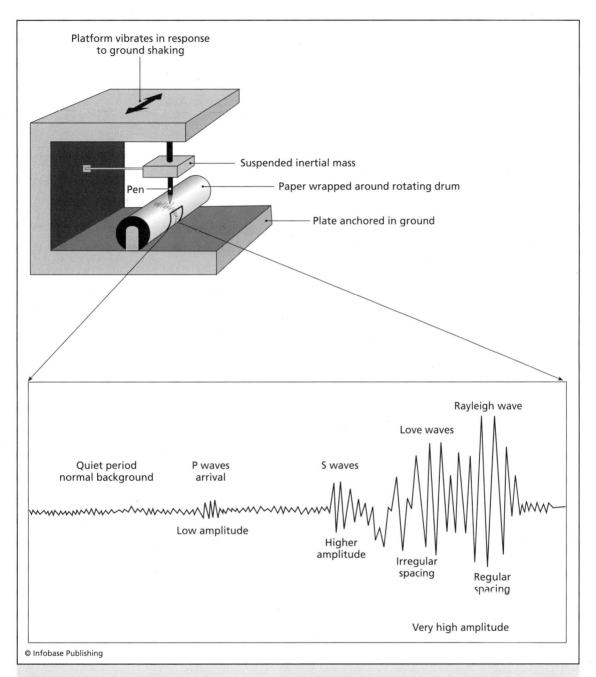

Schematic diagram of an inertial seismograph, showing a large inertial mass suspended from a spring. The mass remains stationary as the ground and paper wrapped around a rotating drum move back and forth during an earthquake, creating the seismogram.

Seismographs are devices that are built to measure the amount and direction of shaking associated with earthquakes. To measure the shaking of the Earth during a quake, the point of reference must be free from shaking, ideally on a hovering platform. Since building perpetually hovering platforms is impractical, engineers have designed an instrument known as an inertial seismograph. This makes use of the principle of inertia, which is the resistance of a large mass to sudden movement. When a heavy weight is hung from a string or thin spring, the string can be shaken and the big heavy weight will remain stationary. Using an inertial seismograph, the ink-filled stylus is attached to the heavy weight, and remains stationary during an earthquake. The continuously turning graph paper is attached to the ground, and moves back and forth during the quake, resulting in the zigzag trace of the record of the earthquake motion on the graph paper.

Seismographs are used in series; some are set up as pendulums and some others as springs, to measure ground motion in many directions. Engineers have made seismographs that can record motions as small as one hundred millionth of an inch, about equivalent to being able to detect the ground motion caused by a car driving by several blocks away. The ground motions recorded by seismographs are very distinctive, and geologists who study them have methods of distinguishing between earthquakes produced along faults, earthquake swarms associated with magma moving into volcanoes, and even between explosions from different types of construction and nuclear blasts. Interpreting seismograph traces has therefore become an important aspect of nuclear test ban treaty verification. Many seismologists are employed to monitor earthquakes around the world and to verify that countries are not testing nuclear weapons.

Earthquake Magnitude

Earthquakes vary greatly in intensity, from undetectable ones up to ones that kill millions of people and wreak total destruction. For example, a bad earthquake in 2003 killed 50,000 people in Iran, yet several thousand earthquakes that do no damage occur every day throughout the world. The energy released in large earthquakes is enormous, up to hundreds of times more powerful than large atomic blasts. Strong earthquakes may produce ground accelerations greater than the force of gravity, enough to uproot trees, or send projectiles right through buildings, trees, or anything else in their path. Earthquake magnitudes are most commonly measured using the *Richter Scale.*

Modified Mercalli Intensity Scale Compared to Richter Magnitude		
MERCALLI INTENSITY	RICHTER MAGNITUDE	DESCRIPTION
I-II	< 2	Not felt by most people
III	3	Felt by some people indoors, especially on high floors
IV-V	4	Noticed by most people. Hanging objects swing, dishes rattle.
VI-VII	5	All people feel. Some building damage (esp. to masonry), waves on ponds.
VII-VIII	6	Difficult to stand, people scared or panicked. Difficult to steer cars. Moderate damage to buildings.
IX-X	7	Major damage, general panic of public. Most masonry and frame structures destroyed. Underground pipes broken. Large landslides.
XI-XII	8 and higher	Near total destruction

The Richter Scale gives an idea of the amount of energy released during an earthquake, and is based on the amplitudes (half the height from wave-base to wave-crest) of seismic waves at a distance of 62 miles (100 km) from the epicenter. The Richter scale magnitude of an earthquake is calculated using the zigzag trace produced on a seismograph, once the epicenter has been located by comparing signals from several different, widely separated seismographs. The Richter Scale is logarithmic, where each step of 1 corresponds to a tenfold increase in amplitude. This is necessary because the energy of earthquakes changes by factors of more than a hundred million.

The energy released in earthquakes changes even more rapidly with each increase in the Richter Scale, because the number of high amplitude waves increases with bigger earthquakes and also because the energy released is according to the square of the amplitude. Thus, it turns out in the end that an increase of 1 on the Richter Scale corresponds to a 30 times increase in energy released. The largest earthquakes so far recorded are the 9.2 Alaskan earthquake of 1964 and the 9.5 Chilean earthquake of 1960, and the 9.0 Sumatra earthquake of 2004, each of which released the energy equivalent to more than 10,000 nuclear bombs the size of the one dropped on Hiroshima.

Before the development of modern inertial seismographs, earthquake intensity was commonly measured using the modified Mercalli intensity scale. This scale was named after Giuseppe Mercalli, an Italian priest and professor of natural science at the seminary of Milan who wrote 150 books on seismology and developed this scale in the late 1800s. He was regarded by some in the church as too liberal, and removed from his professorship, but then moved on to the University of Naples and the Vesuvius Observatory. Mercalli died in 1914 in suspicious circumstances, where his strangled and petrol-soaked burned body was found in his apartment that had apparently been robbed before the deadly fire started.

The Mercalli scale (shown on page 81) measures the amount of vibration people remember feeling for low-magnitude earthquakes, and measures the amount of damage to buildings in high-magnitude events. One of the disadvantages of the Mercalli scale is that it is not corrected for distance from the epicenter. People near the source of the earthquake therefore may measure the earthquake as an IX or X, whereas people further from the epicenter might only record a I or II event. The modified Mercalli scale has however proven very useful for estimating the magnitudes of historical earthquakes that occurred before the development of modern seismographs, since the Mercalli magnitude can be estimated from historical records.

Conclusion

Earthquakes occur when energy is suddenly released within the Earth, generating seismic waves that move away from the source at several miles (km) per second. Most earthquakes are caused by the sudden movement of faults and release of energy from the bent and strained rocks along the fault. Other earthquakes are associated with energy release from volcanic eruptions, landslides, and bomb blasts.

Many different types of seismic waves, each associated with different types of movements as the wave moves, are released during earthquakes.

Since these waves have distinctive types of motion and travel at different but known rates, it is possible to measure the difference in arrival time of the first (primary) waves and the second (secondary or shear) body waves. The larger the difference in time between these waves, the farther the observer is from the source of the earthquake, known as the epicenter. The Richter magnitude is a measure of how high the seismic waves would be at a distance of 62 miles (100 km) from the epicenter.

6

Earthquake Hazards

In this chapter individual hazards associated with earthquakes are examined in detail. The energy released by an earthquake sets many processes into action, and may have both short-term and long-term consequences. Some of the hazards take effect immediately, and others may not appear for days, weeks, or months after the event. Earthquakes are associated with a wide variety of specific hazards, including primary effects such as

- ground motion
- ground breaks (or faulting)
- mass wasting
- liquefaction

Secondary and tertiary hazards are indirect effects, caused by events initiated by the earthquake. These may include

- tsunamis
- seiche waves formed by the motion of lakes and enclosed bodies of water
- fires and explosions caused by disruption of utilities and pipelines
- changes in ground level causing disruption of habitats
- changes in groundwater level
- displacement of coastlines
- loss of jobs
- displacement of populations

Financial losses to individuals, insurance companies, and loss of revenue to business can easily soar into the tens of billions of dollars for even moderate-sized earthquakes between magnitude 6 and 7, if they strike in populated areas.

Ground Motion

One of the primary hazards associated with earthquakes is *ground motion* caused by the passage of seismic waves through populated areas. The most destructive waves are surface waves, which in severe earthquakes may visibly deform the surface of the Earth into moving waves. Ground motion is most typically felt as shaking, and causes the familiar rattling of objects off shelves reported from many minor earthquakes. The amount of destruction associated with given amounts of ground motion depends largely on the design and construction of buildings and infrastructure according to specific codes.

The amount of ground motion associated with an earthquake generally increases with the magnitude of the earthquake, but depends also on the nature of the substratum—loose, unconsolidated soil and fill tends to shake more than solid bedrock. The 1989 Loma Prieta earthquake in California dramatically illustrated this phenomena, where areas built on solid rock vibrated the least (and saw the least destruction), and areas built on loose clays vibrated the most. Much of the San Francisco Bay area is built on loose clays and mud, including the Nimitz freeway, which collapsed during the event. The area that saw the worst destruction associated with ground shaking was the downtown Marina district. Even though this area is located far from the earthquake epicenter, it is built on loose unconsolidated landfill, which shook severely during the earthquake causing many buildings to collapse and gas lines to rupture, initiating fires. More than twice as much damage from ground shaking during the Loma Prieta earthquake was reported from areas over loose fill or mud than from areas built over solid bedrock. Similar effects were reported from the 1985 earthquake in Mexico City, which is built largely on old lake bed deposits.

Additional variations in the severity of ground motion is noted in the way that different types of bedrock transmit seismic waves. Earthquakes that occur in the western United States generally affect a smaller area than those that occur in the central and eastern parts of the country. This is because the bedrock in the West (California, in particular) is generally much softer than the hard igneous and metamorphic bedrock found in the East. Harder, denser rock generally transmits seismic waves better than softer, less dense rock, so earthquakes of given magnitude may be more severe over larger areas in the East than in the West. From the perspective of ground motion intensity, it is fortunate that more large earthquakes occur in the West than in the East.

Ground motions are measured as accelerations, which is the rate of change of motion. This type of force is the same as accelerating in a car, where you feel yourself being pushed gently back against the seat while speeding up. This is a small force compared to another common force measured as an acceleration, gravity. Gravity is equal to 32 feet (9.8 m) per second squared or 1g (this is equivalent to the force experienced by jumping out of an airplane).

Ground motion during the 1964 Alaska earthquake induced landslides that caused Fourth Avenue in downtown Anchorage to collapse. Before the earthquake, the sidewalk and street (with cars) was at the same level as the street on the right. The street collapsed 11 feet (3.4 m) vertically and slid 14 feet (4.3 m) horizontally during the earthquake. *(USGS)*

Landslides from liquefaction associated with excessive ground motion and shaking destroyed the Turnagain Heights neighborhood of Anchorage, Alaska, during the March 27, 1964, magnitude 9.2 earthquake. *(USGS)*

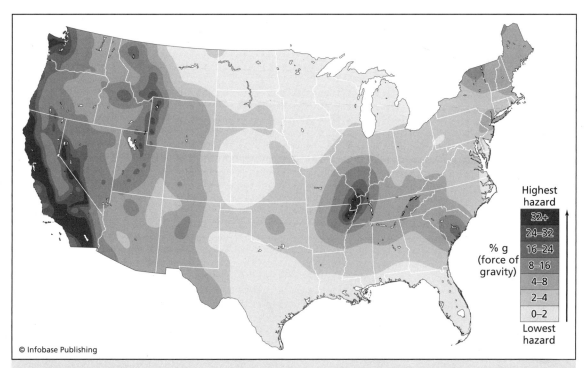

Earthquake hazard map for the United States, showing areas most prone to having severe earthquakes. The label *g* refers to the percentage of the force of gravity that is reached by the force of the earthquake: 100 percent would be as strong as gravity, 50 percent half as strong, etc. Shading corresponds to areas that are likely to experience forces of acceleration that are up to as strong as indicated. *(Modeled after a USGS map)*

People have trouble standing up, and buildings begin falling down at 1/10 the acceleration of gravity. Large earthquakes can produce accelerations that are double or even three times as strong as the force of gravity. These accelerations are able to uproot large trees and toss them into the air, shoot objects through walls and buildings, and cause almost any structure to collapse.

Some of the damage typically associated with ground motion and the passage of seismic waves includes swaying and pancaking of buildings. During an earthquake, buildings may sway with a characteristic frequency that depends on the building's height, size, construction, underlying material, and intensity of the earthquake. This causes heavy objects to slide rapidly from side to side inside the buildings, which can be quite destructive. The shaking generally increases with height, and in many cases the shaking causes concrete floors at high levels to separate from the walls and corner fastenings, causing the floors to progressively fall or pancake upon another, crushing all in between. With higher amounts of shaking the entire structure may collapse.

Ground Breaks

Many adventure or horror movies show earthquakes that include pictures of great ruptures opening in the ground, swallowing up all in their path, and then closing again. Although these scenes are far from reality, ground ruptures are a serious hazard associated with earthquakes.

The Hanning Bay fault on Montague Island in Prince William Sound, Alaska, was reactivated during the March 27, 1964, earthquake. The trace of the fault is marked by a 10 to 15 foot (3–4.5 m) high bedrock scarp that trends obliquely across this photo from lower right in the foreground to upper middle left in the background. The fault trace lies between the uplifted wave cut surface that is coated white by dried up calcareous marine organisms and borders the open ocean and the area of sand and silt in the cove. The ground northwest of the fault (on the right) was displaced as much as 16 feet (5 m) with respect to the ground to the left of the fault, and both sides were uplifted relative to sea level. View is to the southwest. *(USGS)*

Ground breaks or ruptures form where a fault cuts the surface, and may also be associated with mass wasting, or the movements of large blocks of land downhill. These ground breaks may have horizontal, vertical, or combined displacements across them and may cause considerable damage. Fissures that open in the ground during some earthquakes are mostly associated with the mass movement of material down slope, and not with the fault trace itself breaking the surface. For instance, in the 1964 Alaskan earthquake ground breaks displaced railroad lines by several yards, broke through streets, houses, storefronts, and other structures and caused parts of them to drop by several yards (m) relative to other parts of the structure. Most of these ground breaks were associated with slumping, or movement of the upper layers of the soil downhill towards the sea. Ground breaks are also one of the causes of the rupture of pipelines and communication cables during earthquakes.

Mass Wasting

Mass wasting is the movement of material downhill. In most instances, mass wasting occurs by a slow gradual creeping of soils and rocks downhill, but during earthquakes large volumes of rock, soil, and all that is built on it may suddenly collapse in a landslide. Earthquake-induced landslides occur in areas with steep slopes or cliffs, such as parts of California, Alaska, South America, Turkey, and China. One of the worst recorded earthquake-induced landslides occurred in the 1970 magnitude 7.8 earthquake in Peru, in which at least 18,000 people were killed.

In the 1964 magnitude 9.2 earthquake in Alaska, landslides destroyed power plants, homes, roads, and railroad lines. Some landslides even occurred undersea and along the seashore. Large parts of the towns of Seward and Valdez in Alaska were sitting on the top of large submarine escarpments and during the earthquake large parts of these towns slid out to sea in giant submarine landslides and were submerged. Another residential area near Anchorage called Turnagain Heights was built on top of cliffs with fantastic views of the Alaska Range and Aleutian volcanoes. When the earthquake struck, this area slid out toward the sea on a series of curving faults that connected in a slippery shale unit known as the Bootlegger shale. During the earthquake this shale unit lost all strength and became almost cohesionless, and the shaking of the soil and rock above it caused the entire neighborhood to slide towards the sea along the shale unit and be destroyed.

Rockslide on the Sherman Glacier, Alaska, induced by the March 27, 1964, magnitude 9.2 Great Alaskan earthquake. The avalanche was formed by the collapse of Shattered Peak in the middle distance. The debris shows flowlines and terminal lobes. *(USGS)*

Liquefaction

Liquefaction is a process where sudden shaking of certain types of water-saturated sands and muds turns these once-solid sediments into a slurry, a substance with a liquid-like consistency. Liquefaction occurs through a process where the shaking causes individual grains to move apart, and then water moves up in between the individual grains making the whole water/sediment mixture behave like a fluid. Earthquakes often cause liquefaction of sands and muds, and any structures that are built on sediments that liquefy may suddenly sink into them as if they were resting on a thick fluid. It was the process of liquefaction that caused the Bootlegger shale in the 1964 Alaskan earthquake to suddenly become so weak, causing the destruction of Turnagain Heights. Liquefaction is also responsible for the sinking of sidewalks, telephone poles, building foundations, and other structures during earthquakes. Another famous example of liquefaction occurred in the 1964 Japan earthquake, where entire rows of apartment buildings rolled onto their sides, but were not severely damaged internally. Liquefaction also causes sand to bubble to the surface during earthquakes, forming mounds up to several tens of feet high known as sand volcanoes, or ridges of sand.

Apartment blocks in Japan tilted by liquefaction *(National Geophysical Data Center)*

Changes in Ground Level

During earthquakes, blocks of the Earth shift relative to one another. This may result in changes in *ground level*, base level, the water table, and high tide marks. Particularly large shifts have been recorded from some of the historically large earthquakes, such as the 1964 magnitude 9.2 Alaskan earthquake and the 2004 Sumatra earthquake. In 1964, an area more than 600 miles (1,000 km) long in south-central Alaska recorded significant changes in ground level, including uplifts of up to 36 feet (11 m), downdrops of more than six feet (2 m), and lateral shifts of several to tens of yards. Areas along the coastline that were uplifted experienced dramatic changes in the marine ecosystem—clam banks were suddenly uplifted out of the water and remained high and dry. Towns built around docks were suddenly located many yards above the convenience of being at the shoreline. Areas that were downdropped experienced different effects—forests that relied on fresh water for their root systems suddenly were inundated by salt water, and were effectively "drowned." Populated areas located at previously safe distances from the high tide (and storm) line became prone to flooding and storm surges, and had to be relocated.

Areas that were far inland also suffered from changes in ground level; when some areas were uplifted by many tens of feet, the water table recovered to a lower level relative to the land's surface, and soon became out of reach of many water wells that had to be redrilled. Changes in ground level, although seemingly a minor hazard associated with earthquakes, are significant and cause a large amount of damage that may cost millions of dollars to mitigate.

Tsunami and Seiche Waves

There are several types of large waves associated with earthquakes, including tsunamis and *seiche waves*. Tsunamis, also known as seismic sea waves, are usually generated from submarine landslides that displace a large volume of rock and sediment on the seafloor, which in turn displaces a large amount of water. Tsunamis may be particularly destructive as they travel very rapidly (hundreds of miles per hour), and may reach many tens of yards above normal high tide levels. The most devastating tsunami in recorded history occurred in 2004, in association with the magnitude 9.0 earthquake in Sumatra. A wave that reached heights locally of 100 feet (30 m) swept across the Indian Ocean, killing more than 283,000 people, mostly in Indonesia, Sri Lanka, and India.

Two other particularly devastating examples include a tsunami generated by a magnitude 8.7 earthquake in the Atlantic Ocean in 1775 that is estimated to have killed more than 60,000 people in Portugal (this number is from Lisbon alone, although the tsunami struck a large section of coastline, and other related tsunamis were reported from North Africa, the British Isles, and the Netherlands). Another tsunami generated in the Aleutian Islands of Alaska in 1946 traveled across the Pacific Ocean at 500 miles per hour (800 km/hour), and hit Hilo, Hawaii, with

Tsunami damage on the waterfront at Moro Bay, from the 1976 earthquake, that resulted in virtual destruction of the beach community. *(USGS)*

a crest 54 feet (16 m) higher than the normal high-tide mark, killing 159 people, destroying approximately 500 homes, and damaging 1,000 other structures.

Seiche waves may be generated by the back-and-forth motion associated with earthquakes, causing a body of water (usually lakes or bays)

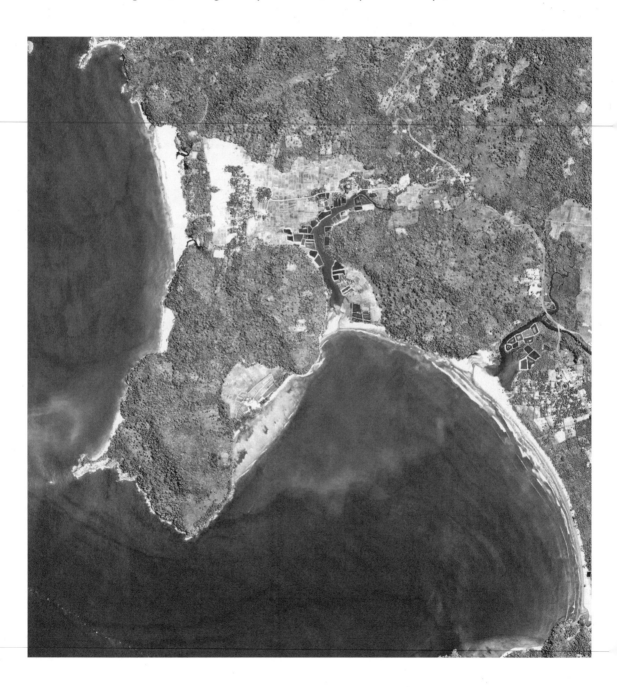

(This page and previous) Two DigitalGlobe satellite images showing coastal community in Aceh, Indonesia, before *(previous page)* and after (below) the 2004 tsunami. Aceh is located on the west coast of Sumatra and suffered some of the worst damage from the 2004 tsunami. Villages and towns were completely destroyed, and most trees, vegetation, and buildings were washed away when the tsunami hit with a height at the shore of more than 50 feet (15 m). Walled-off shrimp farms along the coast (visible as the coastal water-filled pens in the first image) were completely destroyed. The agricultural area behind the town was covered with salt water for days after the tsunami, and sand from the beachfront was completely removed. *(DIGITALGLOBE/EPA/Corbis)*

to rock back and forth, gaining amplitude and splashing up to higher levels than normally associated with that body of water. The effect is analogous to shaking a glass of water back and forth, and watching the ripples in the water suddenly turn into large waves that splash out of the glass. Other seiche waves may be formed when landslides or rockfall drop large volumes of earth into bodies of water. The largest recorded seiche wave of this type formed suddenly on July 9, 1958, when a large earthquake-initiated rockfall generated a seiche wave 1,700 feet (518 m) tall. The seiche wave raced across Lituya Bay in Alaska, destroying the forest and killing several people, including a geologist who had warned authorities that such a wave could be generated by a large landslide in Lituya Bay.

Damage to Utilities (Fires, Broken Gas Mains, Transportation Network)

Much of the damage and many of the casualties associated with earthquakes are associated with damage to the infrastructure and system of public utilities. For example, much of the damage associated with the 1906 San Francisco earthquake came not from the earthquake itself, but from the huge fire that resulted from the numerous broken gas lines, overturned wood and coal stoves, and even from fires set intentionally in order to collect insurance money on partially damaged buildings. In the 1995 Kobe, Japan, earthquake, a large percentage of the damage was likewise from fires that raged uncontrolled, with fire and rescue teams unable to reach the areas worst affected. Water lines were broken so that even in places that were accessible, firefighters were unable to put out the flames. In the Northridge, California, earthquake of 1994, bridges and highways were blocked and destroyed, creating problems of access for emergency and other vehicles. The 1964 Alaskan earthquake destroyed railroad lines, shipping and port facilties, and blocked roadways, wreaking havoc on the transportation system across the south central part of the state.

One of the lessons from these examples is that evacuation routes need to be set up in earthquake hazard zones, in anticipation of post-earthquake hazards such as fires, aftershocks, and famine. These routes should ideally be clear of obstacles such as overpasses and buildings that may block access, and efforts should be made to clear these routes soon after earthquake disasters both for evacuation purposes and for emergency access to the areas worst affected.

Conclusion

Earthquakes are associated with very distinctive types of geological hazards. These include primary effects such as ground motion, ground breaks (or faulting), mass wasting, and liquefaction. Secondary and tertiary hazards are indirect effects, caused by events initiated by the earthquake, and sometimes following some time later. These may include tsunamis, fires, damage to utilities, disease, and changes to the livelihood of people and the economics of whole regions.

The initial few minutes of an earthquake event are typically the most destructive, where the passage of seismic waves can knock down buildings, bridges, cause landslides, and break underground gas and water lines. Coastal areas can be struck by earthquake-related tsunamis if the earthquake displaces the seafloor. Areas that experience strong shaking may also be prone to landslides and other mass wasting movements. The amount of shaking and damage to an area is strongly related to the type of underlying substrate material. Some materials such as thick clay and loose fill tend to amplify certain kinds of seismic waves, and can therefore make the earthquake feel larger and last longer than in surrounding areas.

Long-term effects of earthquakes can be as devastating as the short-term effects. Famine, disease, cold, and hunger can follow in the wake of large earthquakes if the region is not set up with an infrastructure that can allow responders to get help to victims. The economic base of ports and industrial regions can be destroyed by earthquakes, and, if not rebuilt, the job base for entire regions can be lost and populations displaced.

7

Earthquake Prediction, Preparation, and Response

Despite the fact that many small earthquakes occur every day somewhere on the planet, and larger events happen every year, it has proven difficult to predict exactly when and where an earthquake will occur, and how large it may be. Earthquake prediction is a relatively young science that has advanced rapidly over the past 100 years, yet still is unable to accurately forecast exactly when an earthquake may occur along a specific section of a fault. This chapter examines different ways of predicting earthquakes, including determining the historic *recurrence interval* of slip along a fault, mapping seismic gaps, studying the paleoseismic record along different segments of the fault, and monitoring unusual phenomena such as electrical and gas discharges, and strange behavior of animals. In order to understand the risk to people in any location, information on the chances of an earthquake of a specific magnitude occurring in a specific interval needs to be considered along with the risk for strong shaking in specific places. This chapter also examines how geologists combine information on the likelihood of an earthquake occurring in an area with information on how the local geology may help to increase or decrease the amount of ground shaking. Shake maps can be produced that show the specific risk to different areas for different types of predicted earthquakes.

Earthquake Statistics
There are hundreds of thousands of earthquakes every year on the planet, but most of these are relatively small events that do not release

large amounts of seismic energy, or are located far from populated regions so do not affect many people. There are only a few large earthquake events each year, and again most of these are typically located in sparsely populated areas. When large earthquakes do strike populated areas, the amount of damage is strongly dependent on the types of buildings and materials used in construction, the population density, and the preparedness of local officials to deal with such catastrophes.

In recorded history there have only been 20 earthquakes that have caused more than 50,000 deaths and only five earthquakes have had magnitudes exceeding 9 on the Richter scale. The earthquake that cost the highest toll in human lives occurred in Shaanxi, China, in the year 1556. Some 830,000 people died when the earthquake hit, when their cliff-dwelling style homes that were cut into wind-blown silt (loess) collapsed. The huge loss of life was thus directly related to the building materials and population density. Likewise, in 1976 in the worst earthquake disaster of the 20th century, more than 242,000 people died in Tang Shan, China, when dual magnitude 7.8 and 7.1 earthquakes leveled the city. In this case, the building materials were mostly unreinforced bricks, again explaining the huge loss of life. In 2004, an earthquake-induced tsunami killed an estimated 283,000 people in numerous countries around the Indian Ocean after a magnitude 9.0 earthquake off the island of Sumatra. Most loss of life in this event however resulted from the enormous tsunami that swept the Indian Ocean, not from the earthquake itself.

Predicting Earthquakes

Knowing when and where an earthquake will occur and how strong it may be could save innumerable lives by giving warning early enough to allow people to make appropriate responses to short and long term threats. Being able to predict earthquakes has therefore been the goal of many geologists and national planners for some time. Some observations have been used to predict in a very general manner which areas are most likely to have earthquakes in specific intervals of time. These include observations of the *recurrence interval* of earthquakes along individual segments of faults, the building up of strain within rocks near faults, mapping of gaps in minor seismic activity along faults (reflecting places where the fault is stuck, or locked, and may slip, causing an earthquake), and observations of minor changes in the physical properties of rocks. Other earthquake precursors are also being studied, including release of gases before earthquakes, releases of electrical energy before earthquakes, and changes in animal behavior in the few hours immediately preceding large earthquakes.

Predicting earthquakes based on recurrence interval is based on the statistics of how frequently earthquakes of specific magnitude occur along individual segments of faults. In many places, the historical records of past earthquakes do not go back very far compared to the typical interval between earthquakes. For instance, most of the seismically active parts of the western United States only have historical records going back a couple of hundred years, and in parts of the eastern United States these records go back somewhat less than 400 years. In many of these places the interval of recurrence for large earthquakes is estimated to be 200–400 years, so it is difficult to obtain an historical record of the reliability of the recurrence interval. In other parts of the world, such as Japan and China, historical records of earthquakes go back more than a thousand years, enabling better documentation of earthquake intervals.

Earthquake forecasting based on recurrence intervals of past events is based on statistics and yields only probabilities of earthquake events happening in certain time intervals. For example, if historical records show that earthquakes of magnitude 7 occur along a segment of a fault roughly every 150 years (perhaps with a 20 year error margin, so that they really occur every 130 to 170 years), and it has been 149 years since the last magnitude 7 earthquake, does it mean that a magnitude 7 earthquake will definitely occur along that segment of the fault in the next year? The answer is no, but that the probability of a magnitude 7 earthquake occurring within the next 10 years is high.

Seismic gaps are places along large fault zones that have little or no seismic activity compared to adjacent parts of the same fault. Seismic gaps are generally interpreted as places where the fault zone is stuck, and where adjacent parts of the fault are gradually slipping along, slowly releasing seismic energy and strains associated with relative creeping motion of opposing sides of the fault. Since the areas of the seismic gaps are not slipping, the energy gradually builds up in these sections, until it is released in a relatively large earthquake. If the size of the seismic gaps can be measured, and the amount of unslipped relative motion on either side of the fault measured, then the size of the impeding earthquake in the seismic gap can be predicted. Predicting when the earthquakes may occur in seismic gaps is another matter, and estimates must be based on recurrence intervals from past earthquakes, or predicted from estimates of when the strength of the rock in the fault zone will be exceeded and rupture (associated with the earthquake) will occur.

Some of the physical properties of rocks in fault zones actually change in measurable ways prior to some earthquakes, and monitoring of these changes may also ultimately help predict impending earthquake events. One measurable change in rocks is called *dilation,* where the rock expands because of the development of numerous minor cracks or fractures in the rocks that form in response to the stresses concentrated along the fault zone. The amount of dilation may be expressed by surface bulging along the fault zone. In theory, if the strength of rocks in a fault zone is known, and if the stress across the fault zone is known, then the amount of dilation can be related to the decrease in rock strength and an estimate of when the earthquake may occur can be made. Other physical properties of the rocks in fault zones may also change prior to earthquakes. For instance, the velocity of seismic waves is known to change in fault zones prior to some earthquakes, and is thought to reflect changes in the number of small cracks in the rock as the strain accumulates before rupture events. The electrical conductivity may likewise also change, and may also be related to changes in the physical properties of the rocks.

Sometimes large earthquakes are preceded by distinctive swarms of small earthquakes known as foreshocks. These are related to the formation of many small cracks, and may be associated with the tilting of the land surface because of the built-up strain in the rocks adjacent to the fault. With the establishment of seismic monitoring stations near active faults, these small earthquake swarms can be observed and can ultimately help warn of impending large earthquake events.

There are several other poorly understood phenomena that may someday be used to help predict earthquakes. For example, it has been documented in some cases that radon gas levels increase in some groundwater wells before some earthquakes. Groundwater levels in wells may also drop before earthquakes, which may be related to the water filling up the many microcracks that form in the fault zone rocks before major earthquake events. Perhaps most peculiar among earthquake precursors is anomalous animal behavior. Some dogs and horses have exhibited unusual and erratic behavior before some earthquakes, as have snakes, chickens, and fish that leap from the water of ponds. Why these animals behave so unusually before earthquakes is unknown, but may be related to their senses being able to identify changes in gases, light emitted from highly-strained crystals before earthquakes, or to changes in the local electromagnetic field immediately before large earthquakes. Perhaps these animals hold the key to short-term prediction of earthquakes, and we will be able to learn from observing them more closely and analyzing what it is in the environment that they sense changing, before catastrophe strikes.

CHINA'S LIAONING EARTHQUAKE: SUCCESSFUL EARTHQUAKE PREDICTION

Earthquake prediction is a juvenile science that is still attempting to understand specific changes that occur in rocks, soils, water, and the atmosphere both immediately before and for long times preceding large earthquakes. There is one outstanding example of where an earthquake was successfully predicted well in advance, saving thousands of lives. Liaoning Province in northeastern China began to experience swarms of small earthquakes in early 1974, but had not had a major earthquake in more than 100 years. Chinese seismologists were puzzled, and began to investigate and found also that the land surface had been uplifted and tilted toward the west, and that the strength of Earth's magnetic field was changing and growing stronger. The Chinese Seismological Bureau issued a long-range earthquake forecast based on these measurements, stating that the region should expect a moderate sized earthquake within two years. Then on December 22, 1974, a swarm of small earthquakes was centered around the major port city of Yingkou, so the Seismological Bureau revised their forecast to be specific, stating that the Yingkou region should expect a magnitude 6 earthquake within the next six months.

Residents of Liaoning noticed that animals in the region began to act strangely. Pigs chewed off their tails, rats became aggressive toward humans, and snakes came out of hibernation in the depths of winter only to freeze on the surface. Water wells in the area started to bubble with gases rising from depth. Then on February 4, a magnitude 4.8 earthquake shook the area, and was followed by a freeze in all seismic activity. Authorities from the Seismological Bureau understood this to be a foreshock, and ordered 3 million people out of their homes to spend the night outside in the frigid North China winter. At 7:36 P.M. the large earthquake struck. The cities of Yingkou and neighboring Haicheng were destroyed, but instead of tens or hundreds of thousands of deaths, there were only 300 due to the successful earthquake prediction.

Despite the confidence the Chinese felt after this successful prediction and saving of many lives, another earthquake soon struck northern China that was not predicted, resulting in one of the highest death tolls ever recorded from an earthquake. In July 1976, the city of Tang Shan, an industrial city of 1 million people located 100 miles (160 km) east of Beijing was suddenly and unexpectedly hit by a magnitude 7.8 earthquake at 3:43 A.M., while residents were sleeping in their beds. The city was virtually destroyed, and at least 242,000 people were killed; some estimates place the death toll much higher, closer to 800,000, but the Chinese government released few statistics in those days. The Tang Shan earthquake illustrated the widely different types of behavior that characterize earthquakes. Some may be shouting out warnings that they are going to break and these warnings should be heeded. Other earthquakes occur without any warning, as if the ground just snaps. A huge amount of current research around the world is aimed at understanding these differences, and at trying to improve earthquake prediction to save lives.

Seismic Hazard Zones and Risk Mapping

One of the ways to make the public and private sectors aware of the specific risks of earthquakes in individual areas is known as seismic risk zone mapping. In this technique, geologists assess the likelihood of having earthquakes of specific magnitudes in an area, then put together knowledge of how the earth materials in a region or small area will respond to seismic shaking to make a map of likely effects throughout the region or area. These maps incorporate information such as the nature of the underlying rock because different rock types respond to the passage of seismic waves in different ways. For example, thick clay and soil tends to amplify seismic waves, creating longer, more intense shaking than on solid bedrock. The information in seismic risk maps is used by planners for designing further construction, and may also be used with knowledge of population distributions, types of existing structures and utilities to formulate emergency plans before large earthquakes occur. This type of planning can greatly reduce casualties from earthquakes.

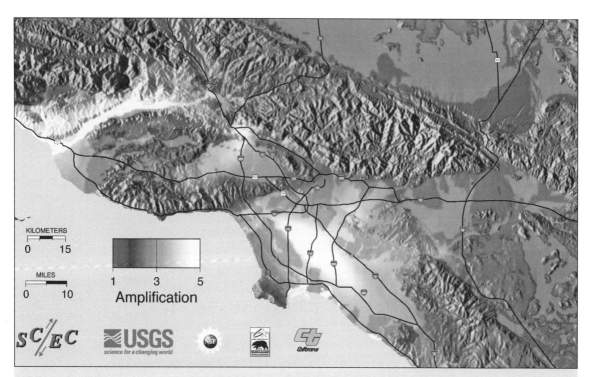

Shake map, produced by the U.S. Geological Survey (USGS) and the Southern California Earthquake Center (SCEC), showing how the level of shaking is likely to vary across the Los Angeles Basin in a major earthquake because of soft sediments and subsurface geologic structures. *(USGS map)*

Paleoseismicity: Understanding Ancient Earthquakes

Earthquakes may occur along major plate boundary faults with a fairly regular repeat time, known as recurrence interval. This is because the plates are sliding past each other along these faults at a very specific rate, and earthquakes occur when the elastic strain, or amount of unaccommodated slip along the fault reaches a critical level. When this critical level is reached the fault breaks and slips, causing an earthquake, and releasing the built up stresses and elastic strain. Geologists can calculate the approximate recurrence interval of earthquakes using fault slip rates and rock strength information. For instance, if the plate motion moves blocks on either side of the fault past each other at one inch (2.5 cm) per year, and the rocks can hold 100 inches (250 cm) of bending and strain before they snap, then after 100 years the fault is likely to snap forming an earthquake. This idea of recurrence interval has been tested in a few places like eastern China, Japan, and the Middle East where historical records go back more than a few hundred years. Unfortunately, in most places like in the United States, historical records only reach back a couple of hundred years at most, shorter than the recurrence interval on most faults. How then can geologists estimate the recurrence interval along specific faults, and make better predictions of the likelihood of earthquakes for particular regions?

The science of *paleoseismicity* attempts to address these problems by interpreting different types of records of ancient earthquakes. Some paleoseismicity studies combine archeology with geology and look for ruins of ancient civilizations that show signs of earthquake damage, and then using isotopic or historical dating methods to determine the time of the ancient destructive earthquake. This technique is used widely in the Middle East, for example in Israel, where thousands of years of habitation and building and destruction has resulted in a rich archeological record. Israel and surrounding nations of Jordan, Lebanon, Syria, Egypt, and Saudi Arabia share a plate boundary with a major fault known as the Dead Sea transform fault, along which Arabia is sliding north relative to Israel and the Mediterranean. Seismologist Amos Nur and colleagues from Stanford University have been active in interpreting paleo-earthquakes from the ruins in Israel and surrounding countries, and have used features like the direction and amount pillars are displaced from their former posts to estimate magnitude and direction of paleo-earthquakes, and dated the ruins to determine the age of these past catastrophic events. They, and others, have suggested that many biblical events such as the destruction of Sodom and Gomorrah could have been caused by great earthquakes, and come up with the scientific evidence to support this view. Many passages in the Bible/Torah discuss earthquakes, so the ancient peoples of these lands were obviously exposed to the phenomenon. Similar paleoseismicity studies are being carried out in eastern China along the Tanlu and other major faults. Much of China's cultural history was however lost during the cultural revolution of Mao Zedong, so interpreting the history of the faulting in this region is more difficult.

Other techniques may be employed to understand ancient earthquakes in places where there are no historical records. Coastlines that are prone to earthquakes often experience a series of uplift or subsidence events associated with each earthquake, and geologists can examine and date features related to each uplift or subsidence event to determine the recurrence interval of large earthquakes. Uplift typically lifts the shallow marine seabed, often a wave cut terrace with communities of clams, mollusks, or other shells, or carbonate reefs above sea level. Since these organisms live in a very restricted zone between high-tide levels and a few meters depth, dating the ages of successively uplifted terraces can yield a pattern of uplift events that correlate with earthquake frequency. Subsidence of coastal regions often results in coastal forests being "drowned," with their root systems exposed to salt water. Dating the successive drowning of coastal forests can tell the geologist the history of subsidence events associated with earthquakes along a coastline.

Other techniques for estimating the recurrence interval on faults are more specific. For instance, geologists who are working to determine the recurrence interval of large earthquakes along segments of the San Andreas Fault are excavating segments of the fault zone, and searching for and finding features that they can relate to past earthquakes. When these features can be dated using isotopic dating methods, a history of movement on the fault can be reconstructed. One of the techniques these geologists use is to find zones of disruption of surface layers, or vertical pipes of sand that fed sand boils and sand volcanoes on the surface during seismic shaking (earthquake) events. Liquefaction of underlying layers causes the sand to intrude through layers of swamp and other sediments in the fault zone, and these sand volcano feeder pipes lead to a layer that was once on the surface at the time of ancient earthquakes. That surface layer is typically disrupted, covered by the sand volcano deposits, then buried by layer upon layer of sediments deposited during quiet times. The geologist trying to determine the recurrence interval along the fault would therefore need to date the horizons of disruption either directly or indirectly (such as by using carbon dating of overlying and underlying carbon-rich peat deposits) and could then determine the recurrence interval for that segment of that fault.

Architecture and Building Codes

Places that are particularly prone to earthquakes should have strict building codes with buildings and other structures designed to withstand the shaking and jolting that accompany earthquakes. Skyscrapers can be constructed to sway, and smaller structures can be built with expansion joints and reinforced concrete so that they can better withstand the passage of the seismic waves. Bridges, tunnels, and pipelines should have the ability to expand and contract, and to vibrate back and forth so that they do not rupture or collapse in earthquakes. Many of these expensive yet important construction features are commonly implemented in Western countries such as the United States where earthquakes are common. In many other parts of the world there are unfortunately no enforced building codes in earthquake zones, and there is accordingly a much greater loss of life associated with property destruction during earthquakes. This was dramatically illustrated by the 1999 magnitude 7.4 earthquake in Izmit, Turkey, during which much of the old parts of the cities in western Turkey survived the earthquake with little damage and loss of life. In contrast, recent, hastily built suburbs and apartment blocks that were built in violation of existing codes collapsed, causing tremendous destruction and loss of life.

There is great variation in the types of materials and style of construction that must be used to build earthquake-resistant structures. For instance, if a building is erected on solid bedrock close to likely epicenters, it should be made to withstand high frequency shaking. The building should be made of flexible material and designed with a tall frame, so that the natural frequency of the short-period shaking does not match that of the building height, amplifying the effect. If the building is constructed on thick unconsolidated sediments, then relatively short, stiff buildings may be the safest structures. In addition to these considerations, many variations in the design of floors, roofs, trusses, shear walls, and frames can greatly improve the chances for a building to survive an earthquake, and for lives to be saved. Other design features have recently been implemented in some cases, including methods to effectively isolate the building from its foundation by adding layers of rubber, ball bearings, and even wheels!

Agencies That Deal with Earthquakes

The U.S. Geological Survey coordinates monitoring of more than 2,500 seismograph stations in the United States, forming a network known as the United States National Seismograph Network (USNSN). These are grouped in Regional Seismograph Networks (RSNs) operated by local institutions, and information collected from these is sent to the National Earthquake Information Center (NEIC) in Colorado, where it is made available for distribution. After an earthquake, the NEIC rapidly reports and updates federal, state, and local emergency coordinators, utilities, the media, and the public. The U.S. Geological Survey works with the NEIC and RSNs to rapidly interpret earthquake magnitude and assists in disaster response in coordination with local authorities. This can include identification of areas that have experienced the most intense seismic waves, areas that may be prone to tsunamis, and warning responders of utilities and nuclear power plants and other facilities that may require special attention. These efforts are coordinated with local authorities including fire and police, as well as national teams including Federal Emergency Management Agency (FEMA), the National Guard, and the Red Cross.

The U.S. Geological Survey also works with local RSNs, government and academic geologists to make seismic risk maps, which are used during earthquake disaster relief to quickly identify and assist areas that may be the worst affected, and require the most rapid attention.

Earthquake Response

Immediately after a disaster, residents of local communities may be in charge of their own safety and well being, and for assisting less-able neighbors. Soon afterwards, local police, fire, and rescue teams will be in charge of rescue operations, search and recovery, evacuations, and establishing centers to go to for fresh water and food. In the case of particularly large or disastrous events, the National Guard or other military units may participate in the rescue operations, establishing communication and hospital services. Hotlines and bulletin boards may be set up to reunite families separated when the earthquake struck. These teams will be in constant contact with scientific teams who will be monitoring aftershocks. In most cases the FEMA will step in at this stage, and begin to take orderly charge of the rescue and cleanup operations. They will work closely with the Red Cross, and also help to organize the massive assessment of damage costs by the insurance companies and banks.

Some extremely sophisticated earthquake warning systems, that warn residents and shut down critical infrastructure such as nuclear plants, are being developed for places including southern California. These warning systems may be able to alert residents or occupants of part of the region that a severe earthquake has just occurred in another part of the region, and that they have several or several tens of seconds to take cover. The thought is that if structures are adequately constructed, and if people have an earthquake readiness plan already implemented, they will know how and where to take immediate cover when the warning whistles are sounded, and that this type of system may be able to save numerous lives.

Utilities Infrastructure and Emergency Response

Experience in disaster mitigation has shown that many lives are lost because emergency response teams have not been ready for large destructive earthquakes. Although it is virtually impossible to have disaster teams ready to handle the largest of earthquakes, municipalities should have plans in place to deal with massive building collapses, large numbers of casualties, and large numbers of displaced people. Special consideration also needs to be given to nuclear and other power plants, high-voltage transmission lines, large pipelines, and aqueducts. This planning needs to be done for times when many roads may be impassable, electricity and gas lines may be shut off, fresh water and food may be unobtainable, and communication could be difficult. Many countries have such plans in place, and several international teams of rapid-response earthquake relief crews have been formed, which has helped immensely following several recent earthquakes. These plans need to be continuously revised, tested, and improved, and they serve as examples for less-developed countries that are just forming such plans.

Earthquake Readiness

For people who live in an area prone to earthquakes, or in an area identified by the U.S. Geological Survey or other agency as an area of high seismic risk, the best way to insure personal safety is to be prepared. Residents do not need to plan daily activities in fear of or in preparation for an earthquake. It is wise, however, to plan homes, classrooms, and offices so that large heavy objects will not tumble on beds or heads, or into other places where people spend large amounts of time, and to take precautions such as attaching heavy furniture to walls. Individuals need to avoid purchasing properties that do not have adequate construction, and look out for areas along steep hillsides that may fail or slump during an earthquake. If there is a choice, it is best to locate homes in areas that do not have thick, unconsolidated sediments, and certainly not on loose fill. Residents of earthquake prone areas should have a battery-operated radio, flashlight, first aid kit, water, and other emergency supplies stored in their homes, in places that are accessible in dark, possibly damaged structures. Communities and families should have plans for meeting up after an earthquake, should members be separated when a large earthquake happens.

Anyone who is in an earthquake should try to get outdoors into an open area after the quake is over and stay away from structures that may collapse, and away from coastlines that may experience tsunamis or seiche waves. People in a crowded city with tall office buildings that may collapse or send glass or other material flying into the street will have to use extreme caution when leaving the building and seeking an open area. Residents should stay away from steep slopes that could collapse. People inside during a quake should generally stay inside for its duration but try to anchor themselves under a strong desk, or in a supported doorway, in a corner, or at least against a wall. They should avoid being next to shelves and heavy furniture that could collapse.

If a major earthquake causes extensive damage to a village, town, or city, it will become critical for survival for people to know what to do after the earthquake is over. First of all, the wounded and trapped must be assisted if possible, and residents should then check their homes for broken gas and water mains, electrical connections, and fires. Remember that most large earthquakes are associated with numerous aftershocks that may be nearly as severe (or, in rare cases, more severe) than the initial earthquake, and buildings that are damaged may be prone to further damage or collapse. Battery-operated radios and cell phones should be located so that small groups can tune to local broadcasts and emergency messages.

Individuals should be prepared to save fresh water as it may quickly become difficult to find—emergency supplies of water may be found in the water heaters of homes, in the cisterns of toilets, from melted ice cubes from the freezer, and in cans of food that are retrievable. In many cases, it is wise to set up camp outside away from buildings that may collapse, and to sleep and cook outside. People should be careful of further building collapse while trying to remove items from homes, and not reenter seriously damaged buildings as they could collapse without warning.

It is often helpful or necessary to organize people from small groups such as city blocks or communities so that everyone can help each other—in severe events it may be days or even a week before organized help arrives and it becomes essential that neighbors work together to help each other, and to search for missing or injured people. They should know where non-potable water supplies may be located so that these supplies may be used to put out fires, and prepare lists of people and their conditions to help authorities when they do arrive.

Conclusion

Each year a few large earthquakes affect densely populated areas. The effects of the earthquakes vary with earthquake strength, building construction style, the preparedness of the population, and emergency response. When earthquake disasters strike, it may take local and national authorities several days to reach many affected areas, so it is essential that residents of earthquake-prone areas have disaster plans in place, and know where to find essential water, food, and medical supplies. Planning ahead for disaster can save lives. Earthquake warning systems that can shut down trains, nuclear plants, and warn residents are being developed, and many cities and towns across the United States are developing earthquake and disaster plans to improve their response to any disaster that may occur.

Many lives could be saved if earthquakes could be predicted and if structures could be built to withstand the shaking from the passage of seismic waves. Studies of the ancient earthquake record of an area, known as paleoseismicity, can reveal the historical frequency of earthquakes in an area, helping geologists predict the likelihood of when the next earthquake may occur. Engineers and geologists have made considerable progress in these goals over the past centuries, but still have far to go. Certain areas, such as along the San Andreas Fault in California, are known to suffer earthquakes of a specific range of magnitude with a fairly regular frequency. In these areas it is possible to map out areas of certain kinds of rock or soil that are prone to high amounts of shaking during earthquakes, and not build on them. Buildings can be strengthened to be able to withstand the forces up to a limit, so that smaller earthquakes can be tolerated with little damage. A growing trend in earthquake-prone areas is to make earthquake warning systems that can alert residents that an earthquake is happening, so that they have a few seconds to take cover before the seismic waves hit their area. Emergency planning, where municipalities make plans for disasters of various types, is an important and increasingly popular way for local governments to be ready to help citizens in the event of an earthquake, saving lives and reducing suffering.

8

Descriptions of Earthquake Disasters

The amount of destruction from earthquakes depends on the earth-quake magnitude, as well as where and when it occurs, the types of building materials used for construction, population density, pre-paredness of emergency rescue teams, and the underlying geology. Huge numbers of casualities have been associated with some historical earthquakes, whereas other earthquakes have huge numbers of casu-alties for their relatively small magnitude. This section provides some brief descriptions of specific earthquakes to illustrate the variability in their destructiveness. Some of the strongest earthquakes to ever occur, such as the 1964 magnitude 9.2 event in Alaska, were associ-ated with few deaths because they struck in sparsely populated areas. In contrast, smaller events, such as the 2005 magnitude 7.6 Pakistan earthquake, killed more than 75,000 people since it hit a densely pop-ulated area where the home construction standards were among the simplest on Earth. According to the following table, there is about one magnitude 9 or greater earthquake every ten years in the world, and larger numbers of smaller earthquakes that cause less damage. Most *great* (> magnitude 8) *earthquakes* occur along convergent margins; other large earthquakes occur along transform margins, and in plate interiors. Divergent margins are generally characterized by smaller temblors. The most dangerous places in the world for earthquake hazards are, therefore, densely populated regions along convergent boundaries, where local construction techniques are substandard.

The 10 Strongest Earthquakes (1900–2000)			
PLACE	YEAR	DEATHS	ESTIMATED RICHTER MAGNITUDE
Concepción, Chile	1960	3,000 deaths	9.5
Valdez, Alaska	1964	131 deaths	9.2
Alaska	1957		9.1
Sumatra	2004	283,000 deaths	9.0
Kamchatka	1952		9.0
Ecuador	1906		8.8
Alaska	1965		8.7
Assam (Northeast India)	1950	1,526 deaths	8.6
Banda Sea	1938		8.5
Chile	1922		8.5

Earthquakes That Struck Convergent Margins

The world's largest earthquakes, often called "great" earthquakes, with magnitudes larger than 8, and rarely 9, occur along convergent plate margins, especially where one oceanic plate is being subducted beneath a continental plate. This type of configuration leads to huge areas being stressed or "bent" into a position where regions measuring hundreds of miles (km) in length and many tens of miles (km) in depth may suddenly slip in one earthquake event, typically releasing more energy than all the other earthquakes on the planet for many years. For example, the 2004 Sumatra earthquake released more energy than all of the earthquakes on the planet in the past 30 years. In this section some of these huge convergent margin earthquakes are described. In a later section the earthquake risks to regions such as the Pacific Northwest are discussed, as this region is situated above a convergent margin subduction zone that may be on the verge of slipping. Likewise, southern California has significant earthquake risks as it is associated with a transform plate margin.

SUMATRA, 2004 (MAGNITUDE 9.2), AND INDIAN OCEAN TSUNAMI

One of the worst natural disasters of the 21st century unfolded on December 26, 2004, following a magnitude 9.0 (some estimates are as high as 9.3, a three-fold difference in energy released) earthquake off the coast of northern Sumatra in the Indian Ocean. The earthquake was the largest since the 1964 magnitude 9.2 event in southern Alaska, and released more energy than all the earthquakes on the planet in the last 25–30 years combined. During this catastrophic earthquake a segment of the seafloor the size of the state of California, lying above the Sumatra subduction zone trench, suddenly moved upward and seaward by several tens of feet (~10 m). The slip event continued for nearly 10 minutes as the central section of the faulted area moved 65 feet (20 m) and the rupture propagated laterally more than 600 miles (1,000 km). The sudden displacement of this volume of underseafloor displaced a huge amount of water and generated the most destructive tsunami known in recorded history.

Within minutes of the initial earthquake a mountain of water more than 100 feet (30 m) high was ravaging northern Sumatra, sweeping into coastal villages and resort communities with a fury that crushed all in its path, removing buildings, vegetation, and in many cases eroding shoreline areas down to bedrock leaving no traces of the previous inhabitants or structures. Similar scenes of destruction and devastation rapidly moved up the coast of nearby Indonesia, where residents and tourists were enjoying a holiday weekend. Tsunami waves moved up to 12 miles (20 km) inland in northern Sumatra and Indonesia. Firsthand accounts and numerous videos made of the catastrophe reveal similar scenes of horror, where unsuspecting tourists and residents are enjoying beachfront playgrounds, resorts, and villages, and watch as large breaking waves appear off the coast. Many moved toward the shore to watch with interest the high surf, then ran in panic as the sea rapidly rose beyond expectations, and walls of water engulfed entire beachfronts, rising tens of feet (~ 10 m) above hotel lobbies, and washing through towns with the force of Niagara Falls. In some cases, the sea retreated to unprecedented low levels before the waves struck, inducing many people to move to the shore to investigate the phenomena; in other cases, the sea waves simply came crashing inland without warning. Buildings, vehicles, trees, boats, and other debris was washed along with the ocean waters, forming projectiles that smashed at speeds of up to 30 miles per hour (50 km/hr) into other structures, leveling all in its path, and killing more than 283,000 people.

Tourists run from approaching tsunami wave, as a wall of water in the distance approaches a beach in Thailand. The people in this image ran and survived. *(AFP/AFP/Getty)*

The displaced water formed a deepwater tsunami that moved at speeds of 500 miles per hour (800 km/hr) across the Indian Ocean, smashing within an hour into Sri Lanka and southern India, wiping away entire fishing communities and causing additional widespread destruction of the shore environment. Ancient Indian legends speak of villages that have disappeared into the sea, that many locals now understand as relating times of previous tsunamis, long since forgotten by modern residents. South of India are many small islands including the Maldives, Chagos, and Seychelles, many of which have maximum elevations of only a few to a few tens of feet (~ 1–10 m) above normal sea level. As the tsunami approached these islands, many wildlife species and primitive tribal residents fled to the deep forest, perhaps sensing the danger as the sea retreated and the ground trembled with the approaching wall of water. As the tsunami heights were higher than many of the maximum elevations of some of these islands, the forest was able to protect and save many lives in places where the tsunami caused sea levels to rise with less force than in places where the shoreline geometry caused large breaking waves to crash ashore.

Several hours later, the tsunami reached the shores of Africa and Madagascar, and though its height was diminished to less than ten feet (3 m) at this distance from the source, several hundred people were killed in these regions by the waves and high water. Kenya and Somalia were hit relatively severely, with harbors experiencing rapid and unpredictable rises and falls in sea level, and many boats and people washed to sea. Villages in coastal eastern Madagascar, recently devastated by tropical cyclones, were hit by large waves, washing homes and people into the sea, and forming new coastal shoreline patterns.

The tsunami traveled around the world, being measured as minor (inches) changes in sea level more than 24 hours later in the north Atlantic and Pacific. Overall more than 283,000 people perished in the December 26 Indian Ocean tsunami, though many could perhaps have been saved if a tsunami warning system had been in place in the Indian Ocean. Tsunami warning systems have been developed that are capable of saving many lives by alerting residents of coastal areas that a tsunami is approaching their location. These systems are most effective for areas located at distances greater than 500 miles (800 km) from the source region of the tsunami (so that it takes the wave more than one hour to get to those regions), but may also prove effective at saving lives in closer areas. The tsunami warning system operating in the Pacific Ocean basin integrates data from several different sources, and involves several different government agencies. The National Oceanographic and Atmospheric Administration (NOAA) operates the Pacific Tsunami Warning Center in Honolulu. It includes many seismic stations that record earthquakes and quickly sorts out those earthquakes that are likely to be tsunamogenic based on the earthquake's characteristics. A series of *tidal gauges* placed around the Pacific monitors the passage of any tsunamis past their location, and if these stations detect a tsunami, warnings are quickly issued for local and regional areas likely to be affected. Analyzing all of this information takes time however, so this Pacific-wide system is most effective for areas located far from the earthquake source.

Tsunami warning systems designed for shorter-term, more local warnings are also in place in many communities, including Japan, Alaska, Hawaii, and on many other Pacific islands. These warnings are based mainly on quickly estimating the magnitude of nearby earthquakes, and the ability of public authorities to rapidly issue the warning so that the population has time to respond. For local earthquakes, the time between the shock event and the tsunami hitting the shoreline may be only a few minutes. Anyone that is in a coastal area and feels a strong earthquake should take that as a natural warning that a tsunami may be imminent, and leave low-lying coastal areas. This is especially important considering that approximately 99 percent of all tsunami related fatalities have historically occurred within 150 miles (250 km) of the tsunami's origin, or within 30 minutes of when the tsunami was generated.

The magnitude 9.0 Sumatra earthquake that caused the Indian Ocean tsunami was detected by United States scientists who tried to warn countries in soon-to-be-affected regions that a tsunami may be approaching. Despite efforts by some scientists over the past few years, no systematic warning system was in place in the Indian Ocean. Initial cost estimates for a crude system were about $20 million, deemed too expensive by poor nations who needed the funds for more obviously pressing humanitarian causes. When the earthquake struck on a Sunday, scientists who tried calling and e-mailing countries and communities surrounding the Indian Ocean to warn them of the impending disaster typically found no one in the office, and no systematic list of phone numbers of emergency response personnel. Having such a simple phone-pyramid list could potentially have saved tens of thousands of lives. Indian Ocean communities have now set up a tsunami warning system as a response to the 2004 tsunami.

What are the costs versus the benefits of improving tsunami warning systems for United States coastal areas? Which areas are most at risk? Most tsunamis that have and will affect the United States are generated by earthquakes in the Pacific Ocean, along subduction-zone convergent plate boundaries similar to the Sumatra trench that unleashed its fury on December 26. The Pacific has a warning system that can detect the deep waves, and alert waiting personnel immediately of the danger. Like the Indian Ocean, the Atlantic and Gulf of Mexico did not have warning systems until after 2006. Even though the risk of tsunamis in coastal areas around these basins is much lower, the cost of a simple warning system is minor compared to the value our society places on minimizing potential loss of life. Earthquakes generate most tsunamis; however, others are generated by landslides, volcanic eruptions, meteorite impacts, and possibly by gas releases from the deep ocean. Any of these events may happen, at any time, in any of the world's oceans.

The areas in the United States at greatest risk for the largest tsunamis are along the Pacific Coast, including Hawaii, Alaska, Washington State, Oregon, and California. Most of the future tsunamis in these regions will be generated in subduction zones in Alaska, along the western and southwestern Pacific, and most-frighteningly, along the

Cascadia subduction zone in northern California, Oregon, and Washington. This region has experienced catastrophic tsunamis in the past, with geologists recently recognizing a huge wave that devastated the coast about 300 years ago. The reason this area has the present greatest risk in the United States for the largest loss of life and destruction in a tsunami is that it is heavily populated (unlike Alaska), and coastal areas lie very close to a potentially tsunami-generating subduction zone. Tsunamis travel faster than regular wind-generated waves, at close to 500 miles per hour (800 km/hr), so if the Cascadia subduction zone were to generate a tsunami, coastal areas in this region would have very little time to respond. If distant subduction zones generate a tsunami, the Pacific tsunami warning system could effectively warn coastal areas hours in advance of any crashing waves. A large earthquake in the Cascadia subduction zone would however immediately wreak havoc on the land by passage of the seismic waves, and then minutes to an hour later, potentially send huge waves into coastal Washington, Oregon, and California. There would be little time to react. It is these regions that need to invest most in more sophisticated warning systems, with coastal defenses, warning sirens, publicized and posted evacuation plans, and education of the public about how to behave in a tsunami emergency. Other coastal areas should initiate ocean-basin wide warning systems, install warning sirens, and post information on tsunami warnings and evacuation plans. Finally, the nation's general public should be better educated about how to recognize and react to tsunamis and other natural geologic hazards.

What are the lessons to be learned from the tragic Indian Ocean tsunami? People near the sea or in areas prone to tsunamis (as indicated by warning signs in places like Hawaii), need to pay particular attention to some of the subtle and not so subtle warning signs that a tsunami may be imminent. First, there may be warning sirens in areas equipped with a tsunami warning system. When the sirens are sounded, then people in coastal areas need to get to high ground as quickly as possible. People in more remote locations may need to pay attention to the natural warning signs. Anyone who feels an earthquake should run for higher ground, since there may only be minutes before the tsunami hits, or maybe an hour or two. It has to be emphasized that tsunamis travel in groups, with periods between crests that can be an hour or more. Thus, it is very important that people realize that they should not return to the beach to investigate the damage after the first crest passes. If the tsunami-generating earthquake occurred far away, and there is no local ground motion, then there may not be any warning of the impending tsunami, except for the thunderous crash of waves as it rises into the coastal area. In other cases, the water may suddenly recede to unprecedented levels right before it quickly rises up again in the tsunami crest. In either case, anyone who wants to enjoy the beach front should remain aware of the dangers. Those camping in tsunami prone areas should pick a sheltered spot where the waves might be refracted and not run up so far. In general, the heads of bays receive the highest run-ups, and the sides and mouths record lower run-up heights. But this may vary considerably, depending on the submarine topography and other factors.

VALDEZ, ALASKA, 1964 (MAGNITUDE 9.2)

One of the largest earthquakes ever recorded is the "Good Friday" earthquake that struck southern Alaska at 5:36 P.M. on Friday, March 27, 1964, second in the amount of energy released only to the 1960 Chile earthquake (at the time of this writing, the 2004 Sumatra earthquake magnitude is still being debated, and will be between 9.0 and 9.3). The energy released during the Valdez earthquake was more than the world's largest nuclear explosion, and greater than the Earth's total average annual release of seismic energy yet, remarkably, only 131 people died during this event. Damage is estimated at $240 million (1964 dollars), a remarkably small figure for an earthquake this size. During the initial shock and several other shocks that followed in the next one to two minutes, a 600-mile (1,000-km) long by 250-mile (400-km) wide slab of subducting oceanic crust slipped further beneath the North American crust of southern Alaska. Ground displacements above the area that slipped were remarkable—much of the Prince William Sound and Kenai Peninsula area moved horizontally almost 65 feet (20 m), and moved upwards by more than 35 feet (11.5 m). Other areas more landward of the uplifted zone were down dropped by several to ten feet. Overall, almost 125,000 square miles (200,000 km^2) of land saw significant movements upwards, downwards, and laterally during this huge earthquake.

The ground shook in most places for three to four minutes during the March 27, 1964, earthquake, but lasted for as much as seven minutes in a few places such as Anchorage and Valdez where unconsolidated sediment and fill amplified and prolonged the shaking. In contrast, ground shaking during the 1906 San Francisco earthquake lasted less than one minute. In the 24 hours after the main earthquake rupture, 28 large aftershocks (10 larger than magnitude 6) hit the region, with epicenters distributed in an area about 50–60 miles (80–100 km) across. The aftershocks continued for months, gradually diminishing in strength but with more than 12,000 aftershocks stronger than 3.5 measured over the next three months.

The shaking caused widespread destruction in southern Alaska, damage as far away as southern California, and induced noticeable effects across the planet. Entire neighborhoods and towns slipped into the sea during this earthquake, and ground breaks, landslides, and slumps were reported across the entire region. The Hanning Bay fault on Montague Island, near the epicenter, broke through the surface forming a spectacular fault scarp with a displacement of more than 15 feet (3 m), uplifting beach terraces and mussel beds above the high water mark, many parts of which rapidly eroded to a more stable configuration. Urban areas such as Anchorage suffered numerous landslides and slumps, with tremendous damage done by translational slumps where huge blocks of soils and rocks slid on curved faults down slope, in many cases toward the sea. Houses ended up in neighbors' backyards, and some homes were split in two by ground breaks. A neighborhood in Anchorage known as Turnagain Heights suffered extensive damage when huge sections of the underlying ground slid toward the sea on a weak layer in the bedrock known as the Bootlegger Shale, which lost cohesion during the earthquake shaking. Tsunamis swept across many towns that had just seen widespread damage by building collapses— washing buildings, vehicles, trains, petroleum tank farms, and anything in its path to higher ground. Near Valdez, a tsunami broke large trees leaving only stumps more than 100 feet (30 m) above high tide mark. Other tsunamis swept across the Pacific destroying marinas as far away as southern California.

The transportation system in Alaska was severely disrupted by the earthquake. All major highways and most secondary roads suffered damage to varying degrees—186 of 830 miles (300 of 1,340 km) of roads were damaged, and 83 miles (125 km) of roadway needed replacement. Seventy-five percent of all bridges collapsed, became unusable, or suffered severe damage. Many railroad tracks were severed or bent by movement on faults, sliding and slumping into streams, and other ground motions. In Seward, Valdez, Kodiak, and other coastal communities, a series of 3–10 tsunami waves tore trains from their tracks, throwing them explosively onto higher ground. The shipping industry was devastated, which was especially difficult as Alaskans used shipping for more than 90 percent of their transportation needs, and the main industry in the state is fishing. All port facilities in southern Alaska except those in Anchor-

Damage along the Seward waterfront after the tsunami and submarine landslides *(USGS)*

age were totally destroyed by submarine slides, tsunamis, tectonic uplift and subsidence, and by earthquake-induced fires. Huge portions of the waterfront facilities at Seward and Valdez slid under the sea during a series of submarine landslides, resulting in the loss of the harbor facilities and necessitating the eventual moving of the cities to higher, more stable ground. Being thrown to higher ground destroyed hundreds of boats, although no large vessels were lost. Uplift in many shipping channels formed new hazards and obstacles that had to be mapped to avoid grounding and puncturing hulls. Downed lines disrupted communication systems, and initial communications with remote communities were taken over by small independently powered radio operators (if a similar event were to happen today, communications would likely be by cell phone). Water, sewer, and petroleum storage tanks and gas lines were broken, exploded, and generally disrupted by slumping, landslides, and ground movements. Residents were forced to obtain water and fuel that was trucked in to areas for many months while supply lines were restored. Ground water levels generally dropped, in some cases below well levels, further compounding the problems of access to fresh water.

After the quake, many agencies had to coordinate efforts to demolish unrepairable structures, move facilities and even entire communities out of danger zones, and to rebuild lost buildings, roads, and railways. Municipal governments, state, and federal authorities helped the U.S. Army Corps of Engineers with the reconstruction effort for urban renewal, with the aim of providing affected communities with better land utilization. Some towns, such as Seward, had to be moved completely to higher, more stable ground where entirely new towns were built. Other towns, cities, and rural areas had to reconstruct the infrastructure, including gas pipelines, roads, railroad tracks, and private homes of thousands of people. Soils were tested for liquefaction potential, and homes were moved away from locations of high liquefaction potential. Areas with high landslide risks were avoided, as were coastal areas prone to tsunamis. All of these efforts resulted in reconstruction of the communities of southern Alaska, so that now they are safer places to live and work. However, since the area is now much more densely populated than it was in 1964, future earthquakes that even approach the strength of the 1964 earthquake are likely to do more damage, and kill more people than that catastrophe.

SOUTHERN CHILE, 1960 (MAGNITUDE 9.5)

The largest earthquake ever recorded struck the Concepción area of southern Chile on May 22, 1960. This was a subduction zone earthquake, and a huge section of the downgoing oceanic slab moved during this and related precursors and aftershocks spanning a few days. The main shock was preceded by a large foreshock at 2:45 P.M. on Sunday, May 22, which was fortunate because this foreshock scared most people into the streets and away from buildings that were soon to collapse. Thirty minutes later at 3:15 P.M., the magnitude 9.5 event struck and affected a huge area of southern Chile, killing an estimated 3,000 to 5,700 people. Another 3,000 people were injured and 2 million were left homeless in the huge area devastated by this quake and its aftershocks. Massive landslides, slumps, and collapse of buildings occurred throughout the region. The Chilean government estimated property damage to be approximately $300 million. An estimated 600 mile long by 190 mile wide (1,000 km long by 300 km wide) section of the fault separating the downgoing oceanic slab from the overriding plate slipped, allowing the oceanic plate to sink further into the mantle. The area that slipped during this event is roughly the size of California.

The main shock from this earthquake generated a series of tsunamis that ravaged the coast of Chile with 80 foot (24 m) tall waves soon after the earthquake, and these waves raced across the Pacific at 200 miles (320 km) per hour, hitting Hawaii where 61 people were killed and damage was estimated at $75 million. The tsunamis then struck Japan killing 138 people and causing another $50 million in damage. Smaller waves hit the west coast of the United States, causing about $500,000 in damage.

One of the more unusual and unexplained events to follow this earthquake was a massive eruption of the Mount Puyehue volcano 47 hours after the main shock, presumably triggered in some way by the earthquake. Although the relationships between earthquakes and volcanic eruptions is not known, recent observations of many volcanoes around the world has noted a correlation between the passage of seismic waves, even from very distant earthquakes, and an increased amount of volcanic activity. Further research is needed to understand these phenomena.

LIMA, PERU, AUGUST 15, 2007 (MAGNITUDE 7.9)

Lima, the capital of Peru, was hit by a large, magnitude 7.9 earthquake at 6:41 P.M., August 15, 2007, and then by a series of aftershocks ranging up to magnitude 6.3 spread along a 300-mile- (500-km-) long zone. The quake was centered 90 miles (145 km) south-southeast of Lima, offshore from the coastal town of Pisco, 160 miles (258 km) south of Lima. The focus of the quake was at 18.8 miles (30.2 km) depth, along the convergent boundary between the Nazca and South American plates. The earthquake was a thrust-type event that moved the South American plate upward and towards the southwest over the subducting Nazca plate. Shaking from the quake in the capital lasted a long two minutes, and the quake generated a small (1 foot, 0.3 m) tsunami. Damage was the strongest in the capital region and in the towns of Canate, Chincha, and Ica, where at least 337 people were killed, and another 1,350 injured. Numerous buildings were seriously damaged and many collapsed.

This strong earthquake struck in a region that has seen several much larger earthquakes in the past, so damage could have been much worse. Two magnitude 8 earthquakes struck this segment of the South American–Nazca plate boundary in 1908 and 1974, a magnitude 8.2 quake struck near this area in 1966, and an 8.3 quake hit the Arequipa area just to be the southeast in 2001. In 1868 this part of the coast of Peru was hit by a magnitude 9 earthquake that generated a tsunami that killed thousands of people as it swept along the coast of South America.

PAKISTAN, OCTOBER 8, 2005 (MAGNITUDE 7.6)

At 8:50 A.M. on Saturday, October 8, 2005, remote areas of northern Pakistan, north of Islamabad and neighboring Afghanistan, were hit by a major earthquake that caused catastrophic damage to a wide area, largely because of the inferior construction of buildings throughout the region. This earthquake killed more than 86,000 people and injured more than 69,000, leaving about 4 million people homeless as the freezing cold of the Kashmir winter set in to the mountainous region. Worst hit was the Muzaffarabad area in Kashmir, where 80 percent of the town was destroyed and more than 32,000 buildings collapsed. Numerous landslides and rock falls blocked mountain roads so it took many days and even weeks for rescue workers to reach remote areas.

The earthquake was initiated by motion on a thrust fault with the epicenter at 16.2 miles (26 km) depth. The thrust fault is part of a system of faults that formed in response to the collision of India with Asia, forming the Himalaya, Karakoram, Pamir, and the Hindu Kush ranges. The Indian plate is moving northward at 1.6 inches (4 cm) per year, and is being pushed beneath the Asian plate forming the high mountains and Tibetan plateau. Slip on a number of faults accommodates this plate motion, and has formed a series of northwest-southeast striking thrust faults in the Muzaffarabad area. These faults deform young Pleistocene alluvial fans into anticlinal ridges, showing that deformation in the region is active and intense, and the region is likely to suffer additional strong earthquakes.

CHI-CHI, TAIWAN, 1999 (MAGNITUDE 7.3)

On September 21, 1999, a magnitude 7.3 earthquake struck the area near Chi-Chi in western Taiwan, causing widespread destruction across the island. A 53-mile (85-km) long segment of the Cher-Lung-Pu thrust fault ruptured at 1:47 A.M. when most people were sleeping, moving laterally up to 33 feet (10 m) and vertically up to 32 feet (9.8 meters) within 60 seconds. The earthquake released an amount of energy roughly equivalent to 30 times that released by the atomic bomb dropped on Hiroshima, and was the largest earthquake to strike the island in a century. There were 2,333 documented deaths and more than 10,000 people were injured, plus more than 100,000 homes were destroyed with total economic losses topping $14 billion.

The Chi-Chi earthquake was associated with many ground ruptures and surface displacement features, even though the epicenter was located five miles (8 km) below the western foot of the Western Foothill Mountains of Taiwan. New waterfalls were created where the fault rupture crossed rivers, and bridge spans collapsed from movement on unstable river banks, and buildings on one side of the scarps were suddenly raised several tens of feet about their neighbors. Landslides and slumps tilted and destroyed many other buildings, typically sending riverfront buildings crashing into the riverbeds. In one example, more than 1,060,000,000 cubic feet (30 million m³) of a mountain slope slid in the Jiu-Feng Er Shan slide, killing 42 people. Miraculously, a woman and two children were carried more than half a mile (1 km) downhill in the landslide, but survived unscratched. In many places sand and even gravel boiled up from liquefaction of buried sediments, forming ridges and sand volcanoes. Near the Ta-An River along the front of the mountains, the slopes of the mountains were changed forming a new anticline above the thrust fault. The Shih-Kang Dam along the Ta-Chia River collapsed where a strand of the fault crossed the spillways, and

The Shih-Kang Dam was built on the Ta-Chia River in Taiwan in 1974–77, across a branch of the Cher-Lung-Pu fault that ruptured in the September 21, 1999, magnitude 7.3 Taiwan earthquake. The quake raised the south side of the dam by 32 feet (9.8 m) and the north side by 6.5 feet (2 m), rupturing the dam. *(T. Kusky)*

Close-up photograph of the spillway area of the dam that collapsed during the Chi-Chi earthquake on Taiwan *(T. Kusky)*

the southern side of the dam was raised more than 30 feet (9.8 meters), destroying the water supply system for T'ai Chung County. Numerous buildings collapsed, but there are many examples of where one building crumbled and the one adjacent to it was barely damaged. Earthquake engineers are studying the structural differences between buildings that did and did not collapse to help improve building codes in the region.

BAM, IRAN, 2003 (MAGNITUDE 6.7)

Iran sits in the zone of convergence between the Arabian and Asian plates and has numerous mountain ranges that formed by folding and faulting of the rocks in the collision zone. There are many earthquakes in Iran, some of which are extremely destructive and have killed many people. For instance, in 1893, an earthquake in Ardabīl, Iran, killed an estimated 150,000 people, and other deadly earthquakes have stricken most regions of Iran, including the capital, Tehran. On December 26, 2003, the ancient Silk Road walled city and citadel of Bam, Iran, was leveled by a magnitude

6.7 earthquake that struck at 5:27 A.M., killing an estimated 27,000–50,000 people, and injuring more than 20,000. Bam was in a region characterized by high seismicity and many earthquakes. In fact, Bam had survived larger earthquakes in the past during its 2,000-year history without being destroyed, so many scientists were puzzled why a moderate-sized earthquake would totally destroy the city.

The earthquake was preceded by some foreshocks on the afternoon of December 25, but since this area is characterized by high seismicity the residents were not alarmed and did not prepare for what was to come. Many of Bam's residents returned home on Thursday evening,

Satellite image of Bam, Iran, taken one day after the December 26, 2003, magnitude 6.7 earthquake that leveled this ancient city. Note the near total destruction of the mud-brick buildings inside the ancient fortress (lower right part of image). *(NASA Earth Observatory, Space Imaging [December 27, 2003])*

December 25, for the Friday holiday, and were woken at 4:00 A.M. on Friday morning by a strong foreshock that sent many residents into the streets. All seemed calm after a short while, so the residents returned indoors, and most were sleeping at 5:27 A.M. when the main earthquake hit, releasing most of its energy directly below Bam, leveling most of the ancient city that had withstood many earthquakes, drought, and seizure by roving warriors including Genghis Khan. Bam was the oldest walled city, originally founded during the Sassanian period (250 B.C.E.), but much was built in the 12th century, and more in the Safavid period between 1502 and 1722. The walled city included about four square miles (6 km^2) including more than 10,000 buildings, and was surrounded by 38 towers. Most of the buildings were made of mud bricks, clay, and straw and were not reinforced, hence when the shaking was most intense these buildings collapsed, burying the residents inside.

Why was Bam destroyed by a magnitude 6.7 earthquake, when it had survived larger earthquakes in the past? This example illustrates that every earthquake is different in terms of where and how its energy is released, and Bam was fortunate in the past. This event was relatively shallow, and the earthquake focus (the point where the energy was first released) was below Bam, and the energy was focused by the surrounding rock structure directly at the old city, much like sound can be focused or directed by cupping your hands around your mouth, or by walls in a city, or canyons in the wilderness. This earthquake released most of its energy directly toward Bam, causing the city to be destroyed.

KOBE, JAPAN, 1995 (MAGNITUDE 6.9)

The industrial port city of Kobe, Japan, was hit by history's costliest earthquake ($100 billion in property damage) at 5:46 A.M. on January 17, 1995. The 30-mile (50-km) long fault rupture passed directly through the world's third busiest port city and home to 1.5 million people. With little warning, 6,308 people died in Kobe before sunrise on that cold January morning. The rupturing event took 15 seconds, and moved each side of the fault more than six feet (1.7 m) horizontally relative to the other side, and uplifted the land by three feet (1 m). There are many areas of unconsolidated sediment in and around Kobe, and these areas saw some of the worst damage, and shook for as long as 100 seconds because of the natural amplification of the seismic waves. Liquefaction was widespread and caused much of the damage, including collapse of buildings and port structures, and destruction of large parts of the transportation network. Water, sewer, gas, and electrical systems were rendered useless. More than 150,000 buildings were destroyed in the initial quake, and a huge fire that started from ruptured gas lines consumed the equivalent of 70 square blocks.

These examples of convergent margin earthquakes show that the strongest, deadliest earthquakes tend to occur at these convergent margins. Areas thousands of miles (km) long can suddenly slip in one large earthquake event, generating fast-moving seismic waves, giant tsunamis, landslides, shifts of land level, and indirect effects such as fires, disease, and loss of livelihood for millions of people. Convergent margin earthquakes are capable of releasing more energy than any other catastrophic Earth events, and can therefore be among the most destructive forces of nature.

Earthquakes That Struck Transform Margins

Transform plate margins sometimes also have large earthquakes, typically up to magnitude 8. These events can be quite devastating, but are not as big as the magnitude 9+ events that may occasionally strike convergent margins. However, the distinction between a magnitude 9 and a magnitude 8 earthquake will not matter to people who are in collapsing buildings and cities devastated by these massive destructive events. Some plate boundaries have characteristics of both convergent margins and transform margins, such as where a plate is being subducted obliquely, and part of the overriding plate moves sideways along the plate margin. These margins, such as southeastern Alaska, or northern Sumatra—Andaman Islands, may have both subduction zone earthquakes (along the Benioff or subduction zone) and transform margin earthquakes (with the hypocenter located along the transform fault in the overriding plate). Some of the most famous of all earthquakes have occurred along transform plate boundaries. The following is a set of examples that describes some of the more significant earthquakes to strike transform margins in history.

SAN FRANCISCO, 1906 (MAGNITUDE 7.8)

Perhaps the most infamous earthquake of all time is the magnitude 7.8 temblor that shook San Francisco at 5:12 A.M. on April 18, 1906, virtually destroying the city, crushing 315 people to death, and killing 700 people throughout the region. Many of the unreinforced masonry buildings that were common in San Francisco immediately collapsed, but most steel and wooden frame structures remained upright. Ground shaking and destruction were most intense where structures were built on areas filled in with gravel and sand, and least intense where the buildings were anchored in solid bedrock. Most of the destruction from the earthquake came not from ground shaking, but from the intense firestorm that followed. Gas lines and water lines were ruptured, and fires started near the waterfront worked their way into the city. Other fires were inadvertently started by people cooking in residential neighborhoods and by people dynamiting buildings trying to avoid collapses and stop the spread of the huge fire. It has even been reported that some fires were started by individuals in attempts to collect insurance money on their slightly damaged homes. In all, 490 city blocks were burned.

The problems did not cease after the earthquake and fires, but continued to worsen as a result of the poor sanitary and health conditions that followed, as a consequence of the poor infrastructure. Hundreds of cases of bubonic plague claimed lives, and dysentery and other diseases combined to bring the death total to as high as 5,000.

One of the lessons that could have been learned from this earthquake was not appreciated until many years later, that is that loose unconsolidated fill tends to shake more than solid bedrock during earthquakes. San Franciscans noted that some of the areas that shook the most and suffered from the most destruction were built on unconsolidated fill. After the 1906 earthquake, much of the rubble was bulldozed into San Francisco Bay, and later construction on this fill became the Marina district, which saw some of the worst damage during the 1989 Loma Prieta earthquake.

LOMA PRIETA, 1989 (MAGNITUDE 7.1)

The San Francisco area and smaller cities to the south, especially Santa Cruz, were hit by a moderate-sized earthquake (magnitude 7.1) at 5:04 P.M. on Tuesday, October 17, 1989, during live broadcast of the World Series baseball game. Sixty-seven people died, 3,757 people were injured, and 12,000 were left homeless. Tens of millions of people watched on television as the earthquake struck just before the beginning of game three, and the news coverage that followed was unprecedented in the history of earthquakes.

The earthquake was caused by a rupture along a 26-mile (42-km) long segment of the San Andreas Fault near Loma Prieta peak in the Santa Cruz Mountains south of San Francisco. The segment of the fault that had ruptured was the southern part of the same segment that ruptured in the 1906 earthquake, but this rupture occurred at greater depths and involved some vertical motion as well as horizontal motion. The actual rupturing lasted only 11 seconds, during which time the western (Pacific) plate slid almost six feet (1.9 m) to the northwest, and parts of the Santa Cruz Mountains were uplifted by up to four feet (1.3 m). The rupture propagated at 1.24 miles per second (2 km/sec), and was a relatively short-duration earthquake for one of this magnitude. Had it lasted much longer, the damage would have been much more extensive. As it was, the damage totals amounted to more than $6 billion.

The actual fault plane did not rupture the surface, although many cracks appeared and slumps formed along steep slopes. The Loma Prieta earthquake had been predicted by seismologists because the segment of the fault that slipped had a noticeable paucity of seismic events since the 1906 earthquake, and was identified as a seismic gap with a high potential for slipping and causing a significant earthquake. The magnitude 7.1 event and the numerous aftershocks filled in this seismic gap, and the potential for large earthquakes along this segment of the San Andreas Fault is now significantly lower. There are, however, other seismic gaps along the San Andreas Fault in heavily populated areas that should be monitored closely.

TURKEY, 1999 (MAGNITUDE 7.8)

On August 17, 1999, a devastating earthquake measuring 7.4 on the Richter scale hit heavily populated areas in northwestern Turkey at 3:02 A.M. local time. The epicenter of the earthquake was near the industrial city of Izmit about 60 miles (100 km) east of Istanbul, near the western segment of the notorious North Anatolian strike slip fault. The earthquake formed a 75-mile (120-km) long surface rupture, along which offsets were measured between four and 15 feet (1.5–5 m). This was the deadliest and most destructive earthquake in the region in more than 60 years causing more than 30,000 deaths and the largest property losses in Turkey's recorded history. The World Bank estimated that direct losses from the earthquake were approximately $6.5 billion, with perhaps another $20 billion in economic impact from secondary and related losses.

The losses from this moderate-sized earthquake were so high because

- the region in which it occurred is home to approximately 25 percent of Turkey's population
- it hosts much of the country's industrial activity
- it has seen a recent construction boom in which building codes were ignored

- large numbers of high-rise apartment buildings were constructed with substantial materials including extra-coarse and sandy cement
- there were too few reinforcement bars in concrete structures
- there was general lack of support structures.

Earthquakes That Struck Intraplate Regions and Divergent Margins

Most damaging earthquakes are associated with convergent or transform plate margins, as described earlier in this chapter. However, some large earthquakes occur in the interiors of plates and inflict considerable damage, partly because they strike in regions where they are not expected and building codes are not as strict as in more earthquake-prone regions. Most divergent margin earthquakes are relatively small because the lithosphere is weaker in extension (when pulled apart) than in compression (when pushed together) so the stresses are released by faulting in extensional zones well before they have a chance to build up to the levels that characterize the great earthquakes of subduction zones. Some *intraplate earthquakes* appear to be associated with incipient plate boundaries that are just starting to form, others are associated with ancient plate boundaries, which may represent zones of weakness in the lithosphere. Still others seem to occur randomly, representing the culmination of far-field stresses transmitted across continents from distant plate boundaries. The following is a description of the most famous intraplate earthquake sequence to have affected the United States in the past two hundred years, that of the New Madrid earthquakes of 1811 and 1812. After that, descriptions of more recent intraplate earthquakes from Egypt and India are presented.

NEW MADRID (ST. LOUIS), 1811, 1812 (MAGNITUDE 7.6–8.0)

The New Madrid area in the Mississippi River Valley about 100 miles (160 km) south of St. Louis, Missouri, lies very far from any plate boundaries, yet this region was struck by a series of severe earthquakes in 1811 and 1812, well before the region became heavily populated. At 2:00 A.M. on the night of December 16, 1811, a fault deep beneath the river channel ruptured with an estimated magnitude greater than 8, releasing one of the strongest earthquakes ever recorded in the lower 48 states. Aftershocks continued through the night, with another large tremor that was about as strong as the first striking at 7:00 A.M., and an even larger quake hitting at 11:00 A.M. The shocks caused a large area around the Mississippi to subside by up to 15 feet (5 m) forming large swampy areas, including Lake Saint Francis and Reelfoot Lake. An area west of the Mississippi was uplifted about 20 feet (7 m), and the uplift reportedly caused the Mississippi to flow backwards for a short time, and formed short-lived waterfalls on the river. Liquefaction was widespread, with sand boils and sand volcanoes popping up over a wide region. The town of New Madrid on the banks of the river largely disappeared by slumping into the river, and through the subsidence associated with the ground deformation. Shaking, liquefaction, slumping, and other secondary effects of the earthquake were widespread across the Mississippi River Valley area, especially between Memphis and St. Louis. Shaking was felt across the entire eastern United States, and chimneys were toppled in Charleston, South Carolina, Cincinnati,

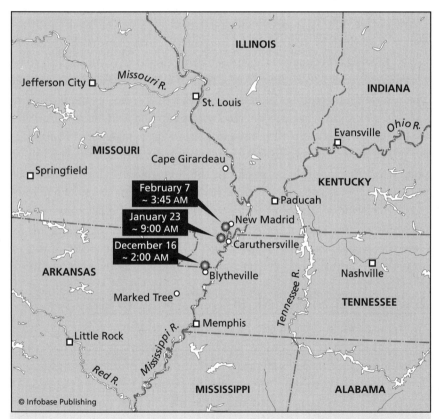

Map of the New Madrid area, central United States, showing the locations of the major shocks of 1811 and 1812 as large dots. Three-dimensional block diagram (opposite page) shows the deep crustal structure that is responsible for the earthquakes in the region. An old rift, named the Reelfoot Rift, lies buried beneath surface rocks, and experiences occasional earthquakes as a result of stresses transmitted across the continent. (Modeled after map from St. Louis University Earthquake Center)

Ohio, and Boston, Massachusetts. Indians in Canada and North Dakota reported feeling the tremors. Luckily, only a few hundred people lived in the region in 1811, so only a few people were killed. If a similar event were to occur today, many more casualties would result because the region is now densely populated. The series of aftershocks continued for sometime, culminating in another large shock on February 7, 1812, that was the largest of all the shocks in the region.

The cause of the New Madrid earthquakes is not as well understood as earthquakes that occur along plate boundaries, but some aspects of the earthquake hazard potential in this area are well known from studies of the many small earthquakes that still occur in the region. The earthquakes occurred along a series of faults that strike parallel to the Mississippi River (the river follows the faults) and represent a deep-seated ancient rift, or place where the crust has ruptured in extension, forming thick deposits of sediments with many faults along the rift margins. This deep-seated rift is a zone of weakness on the scale of the North Ameri-

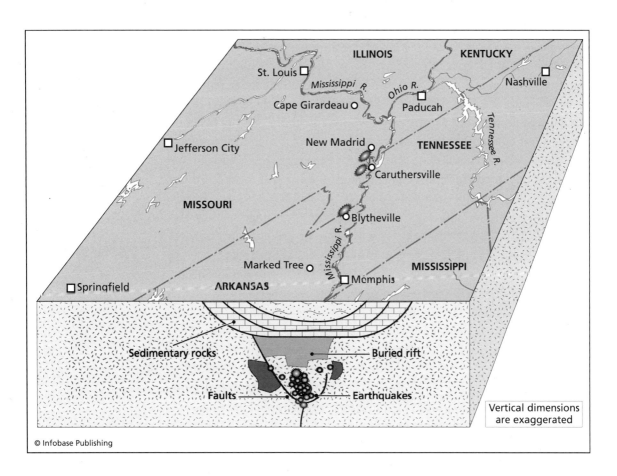

© Infobase Publishing

can continent. When plate boundary stresses are transmitted from far away, this is the first area to break, having faults in favorable orientations for slip. With only a few large earthquakes recorded in the geological record from this area it is difficult to accurately determine the recurrence frequency for large earthquake events along the New Madrid fault, or whether the 1811–12 events may have been isolated events that are unlikely to recur ever. The best estimates currently available are that large earthquakes only strike this region every 400–500 years, with the next event most likely to occur sometime near the year 2310.

Other places in the lower 48 states that are far from plate boundaries have also had significant earthquakes, including Charleston, South Carolina, and Boston, Massachusetts. Charleston is about 1,000 miles (1,600 km) from the eastern boundary of the North American plate along the Mid-Atlantic Ridge, yet it is a moderately seismically active area prone to small to medium sized earthquakes. On August 31, 1886, a major earthquake struck Charleston, killing 60 people. At the time Charleston had a population of 50,000 and the earthquake did an estimated damage of $5.5 million to buildings, railroad lines, and other infrastructure. The earthquake focus is estimated to have been about 13 miles (21 km) deep. Based on the huge area affected by the earthquake—5 million square miles (13 million km^2)—the magnitude of the 1886 quake is estimated to have been a 7.2. The rocks along the East Coast of the United States are harder and transmit seismic waves more efficiently that the bedrock on the West Coast. Therefore, earthquakes of similar magnitude are felt over much larger distances on the East Coast. Interestingly, this quake may have triggered some secondary effects at large distances from the epicenter. For example, natural gas wells in Pennsylvania reportedly showed a drastic reduction in yield as a result of passage of the seismic waves from this earthquake, and a geyser in Yellowstone National Park reportedly sprung to action after many years of inactivity. Such far field effects of large earthquakes are only recently being understood, and much current research is geared toward understanding them.

Large intraplate earthquakes have also struck the New York and New England areas, with large quakes in New York in 1737 and 1884, and 1755 in Boston. A fault north of Boston has recently been determined to be active, and the threat to the city is substantial. One of the biggest threats is that much of Boston, especially the Back Bay region, is built on fill where swamps were filled in with material excavated to make the subway system. The potential exists for massive building collapse if these fills become compacted or liquefied during an earthquake, in a manner similar to the destruction of the Marina district of San Francisco during the 1989 Loma Prieta earthquake in California.

GHUJARAT, INDIA, 2001 (MAGNITUDE 7.7)

The deadliest intraplate earthquake in modern history struck north-western India on January 26, 2001. The people of the Ghujarat region were woken up that morning to a scene of total destruction and the news that 20,005 of their neighbors were killed and another 166,000 injured by a magnitude 7.7 earthquake. January 26 was their Republic Day, a national holiday, which hampered rescue operations. Nearly $5 billion of damage included the loss of 348,000 homes displacing 600,000 people, and damage to another 844,000 homes, mostly in the city of Bhuj. The cause of the Ghujarat earthquake is different from other intraplate earthquakes such as the New Madrid and Charleston earthquakes. In the Ghujarat case, a deep buried thrust or contractional fault known as a blind thrust is thought to be responsible. The thrust fault is a shallow structure with an east-west trace, and is related to stresses generated by the collision between India and Asia. The Ghujarat region has had many smaller earthquakes in the past hundred years, most with magnitudes less than 5. In 1819 another earthquake with 7.7 magnitude hit the nearby Rann of Kachchh area of Ghujarat, killing nearly 2,000 people. The Ghujarat region can therefore expect additional earthquakes, and should take precautions in terms of building codes, better established earthquake disaster management planning, and hazard mapping. Such practices are difficult however, in less developed countries where costs of such preparation can be exorbitant.

DHARSHUR, 1992 (MAGNITUDE 5.9), AND UPPER EGYPT SEISMICITY

Egypt lies on the northeastern edge of the African plate, and the Red Sea forms an extensional plate boundary on its eastern side. Interior parts of Egypt are on what is considered a stable platform with the coastal plain merging with a passive margin on the Mediterranean coast. The Red Sea coast is understandably characterized by many small- to intermediate-sized earthquakes, however, interior parts of Egypt that should be stable have also had a number of historical and recent earthquakes.

The El Faiyum area occupies one of the spectacular depressions in the Eocene limestone plateau of the Western Desert of Egypt. It is located to the west of the Nile Valley, about 60 miles (100 km) to the southwest of Cairo. The El Faiyum depression is separated from the Nile

Photo of buildings destroyed in Cairo's City of the Dead during the October 12, 1992, magnitude 5.9 Dharshur earthquake. The buildings are tombs that house sarcophaguses with ancient mummified remains, although many of the buildings are now inhabited by living relatives of the dead who can not afford the expensive housing in Cairo. This part of Cairo suffered extensive damage in the 1992 quake. *(T. Kusky)*

basin by a water divide and encompasses an area of approximately 2,400 square miles (6,300 km²). Lake Qarun is situated in the northern part of the depression, and has an area of less than 77 square miles (200 km²), with an elevation of 147 feet (45 m) below sea level.

The origin of the depression has been a subject of controversy since Herodotus described the extensive lake in the area in circa 450 B.C.E., known then as Lake Moeris. Some geologists suggested that the lake-filled depression started to form in the middle Pliocene and the beginning of the Pleistocene, with wind erosion operating until the depression attained its present depth. Others assumed that excavation of the depression resulted from a complex action of tectonic movements followed by wind erosion, which actively weathered the fractured rocks. Still others suggested a tectonic origin for the El Faiyum depression and considered it as a crustal sag in the elevated seafloor of the Mediterranean.

On August 7, 1847, a large earthquake with an estimated magnitude of 5.5–5.9 shook the El Faiyum–Cairo region. Hundreds of people were killed and injured, and many thousands of structures were destroyed. The earthquake was felt across Egypt and much of North Africa, with heavy damage reported as far as Assuit in Southeast Egypt. A magnitude 4.8 earthquake shook the area again on January 10, 1920. On October 12, 1992, another large (magnitude 5.9) earthquake shook the Dahshour area, northeast of the El Faiyum region, along a fold belt that

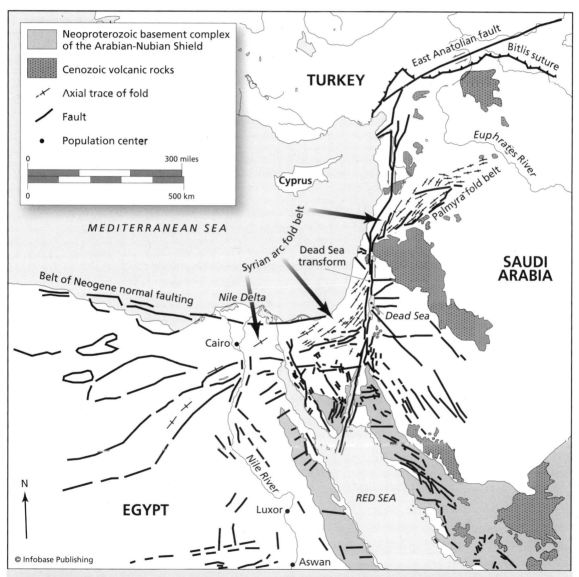

Map of the Syrian arc tectonic belt showing the location of folds and faults across northern Egypt, Israel, Lebanon, and Syria *(Modified from T. Kusky and F. El-Baz, 2000)*

extends into northern Sinai. Heavy damage was reported in the region (including Cairo); hundreds of people were injured and thousands of houses were damaged in different parts of the country. Most recent seismicity in the Sinai Peninsula is related to rifting and strike slip faulting along the Red Sea and Gulfs of Suez and Aqaba, although faulting related to movements along the El Faiyum–North Sinai trend is possible. For instance, on August 23, 1987, a magnitude 3.5 earthquake had an epicenter near Gabal Maghara in North Sinai, far from faults related to the Gulfs of Suez and Aqaba, but along the El Faiyum–North Sinai fold belt. The present seismic activity and well-documented evidence of historical earthquakes in the region, together with the exploration for economic petroleum deposits in the Qarun oil field, has led to a greater understanding of the structural geology of the El Faiyum depression.

Recent work has shown that the El Faiyum depression is part of the southwestern end of the Syrian arc fold belt that stretches from the Euphrates River through the Palmyra fold belt in Syria, through the Levantine fold belt in Israel, across the northern Sinai Peninsula, and across the Nile River past the Giza plateau into the El Faiyum depression of Egypt, and into the Gabal Akhdar area in Libya. The Syrian arc fold belt is characterized by groups of related structures including folds, faults, uplifts, and depressions. In the El Faiyum–Cairo–North Sinai part of the fold belt, deformation began in the Cretaceous, and ended for the most part in the Eocene. Less intense deformation and uplift, however, probably continues through the present day, as demonstrated by historical and recent earthquakes, uplifted Holocene beach terraces between Bardawil Lagoon and Gebel Maghara, and fault scarps cutting recent alluvium in north-central Sinai. The Cairo–El Faiyum area has a well-documented historical earthquake record that demonstrates probable activity in the belt of faults and folds that extends into the northern Sinai Peninsula.

The origin of the seismicity in northern Egypt is not certain. However, one possibility is that the El Faiyum depression, and particularly Lake Qarun, may have formed as a pull-apart basin during dextral shear along the Syrian arc fold belt, related to the rotation of Arabia away from Africa about a pole of rotation in North Africa. In this scenario, Lake Qarun would be situated along an extensional bend in the strike-slip fault system, consistent with the right step in the pattern of major faults from the southern to the northern side of Lake Qarun. Further work is needed to test this hypothesis, although it does appear compatible with relative plate motion vectors for Africa relative to Eurasia in this time interval. The evidence of historical and recent seismicity, together with the structurally controlled escarpments on the northern side of the El Faiyum depression, suggest that the area has potential for significant and destructive earthquake activity.

Conclusion

The most destructive earthquakes have been those that have hit populated areas along convergent plate margins. Recent examples include the 2004 Sumatra earthquake and ensuing Indian Ocean tsunami that killed an estimated 283,000 people, and the 2005 earthquake in Pakistan, along the India–Asia convergent boundary, that killed an estimated 86,000 people. Earthquakes that strike transform plate margins can also be extremely destructive, especially because some transform margins such as the western coast of the United States are densely populated. The most famous transform margin earthquake of all time is the 1906 earthquake and ensuing fire that destroyed much of San Francisco. Descriptions of the 1906 San Francisco earthquake show that the risk to personal health can continue for months after the earthquake, as thousands of people perished in San Francisco from diseases including dysentery and bubonic plague that infested the area after the earthquake, as a result of poor sanitary conditions. Divergent plate margins typically only suffer minor to intermediate strength earthquakes, but some plate interiors have experienced large magnitude events. The most famous example is the series of magnitude 7.5–8.0 earthquakes that hit the New Madrid area in Missouri in 1811 and 1812, which were felt around the country. The New Madrid area was sparsely populated at that time so the damage and loss of life were minimal, but if a similar earthquake were to hit the region today, the densely populated areas of St. Louis and Memphis could suffer major damage.

Summary

Landforms including mountains, plains, valleys, and deep-sea trenches on the surface of the Earth reflect different types of plate tectonic structures. Tall mountains form where plates are colliding, flat plains form in plate interiors, basin and range provinces form in areas that are being extended in divergent boundaries, and deep-sea trenches represent places where an oceanic plate is moving back into the mantle. Studies of these landforms have revealed that there are three main types of plate boundaries. Divergent boundaries are where two tectonic plates are moving apart from each other, and include the mid-ocean ridge system and continental rifts. Convergent boundaries are where two plates are moving towards each other, and include several varieties. An oceanic plate may be pushed beneath another oceanic plate forming an island arc on the overriding plate, or an oceanic plate may be pushed beneath a continent, forming a convergent margin volcanic arc on the continent. Collision zones are places where island arcs or continents are colliding with other continents, such as India with Asia, forming tall mountain ranges like the Himalaya chain. Transform boundaries develop where one plate simply slides past the other along a transform fault, with the most famous example being the San Andreas Fault along the western North America transform boundary.

Most earthquakes occur when stress from the slow movement of plates build up to such levels that the rocks along plate boundaries suddenly break, releasing energy that propagates out in all directions as seismic waves. Large earthquakes release enough energy to uproot trees, knock down tall buildings, and send mountain sides crashing down onto towns below. Specific hazards are associated with the back and forth motion of the ground during the passage of seismic waves; by large cracks that can open in the Earth from faults and movement of the ground; from landslides and related phenomena; and from liquefactions, the conversion of soil into a liquid-like state during intense shaking. Some earthquakes also generate tsunamis, and many cause extensive damage to underground gas and water pipelines that may allow a second wave of destruction comprised of fire and gas explosions to wreak havoc on earthquake damaged cities. The most destructive earthquakes are associated with convergent boundaries, and the least with divergent boundaries. Large earthquakes may also occur along transform boundaries and sometimes in the interior of plates.

Geologists and engineers have spent great efforts in trying to understand and predict earthquakes in order to save lives. Paleoseismicity is the study of ancient earthquake records, and is widely used to determine the repeat or recurrence interval of large earthquakes on specific faults or in certain regions. Knowing the recurrence interval is important to know if earthquakes of certain magnitude happen, for instance, every 100, every 200, or every 400 years along a specific fault. This information can then be used to predict the chances of an earthquake happening any year along that fault. Studies of the rock and soil under an area can be used to tell engineers how much shaking is likely to occur during an earthquake, since some soils amplify seismic waves and buildings constructed on these will shake more during an earthquake than buildings anchored in solid bedrock. Buildings are now being constructed so that they can withstand earthquakes of larger magnitude than those built 50 years ago. Communities and local governments have been devising emergency response plans to be ready to help people who are trapped and injured during major earthquake events. Despite this, it could still take days for help to reach some people in cities that have been hit by severe earthquakes.

Historical accounts of many earthquakes have shown that the amount of death and destruction is closely related to the population density and quality of buildings in an area. If a huge earthquake hits an unpopulated area, it is of little consequence. However, even moderate-sized earthquakes have killed tens and even hundreds of thousands of people in areas where homes are made of unreinforced concrete, piles of stones, or loose earth. Parts of southern California and the Pacific Northwest are deemed the most vulnerable areas in the United States for future large earthquakes in densely populated areas, and residents in these areas need to be diligent in application of strict building codes, development of earthquake warning systems, and in preparation of sophisticated emergency response plans.

As noted, studies of the historical earthquake patterns and population densities show that much of California and the Pacific Northwest are the most at-risk regions in the United States for earthquakes. The current state of the stress build up along faults shows that southern California is most likely to suffer a major earthquake in the next 50 years, although it is currently impossible to tell exactly when this earthquake might strike. Government disaster planners in these regions are devising emergency response plans, and building codes have been improved to make the people and infrastructure in these areas less prone to injury and damage. Further studies and monitoring can continue to improve the science of earthquake prediction, perhaps one day saving thousands of lives.

Appendix

The Geologic Timescale

Era	Period	Epoch	Age (millions of years)	First Life-forms	Geology
		Holocene	0.01		
	Quaternary				
		Pleistocene	3	Humans	Ice age
Cenozoic		Pliocene	11	Mastodons	Cascades
		Neogene			
		Miocene	26	Saber-toothed tigers	Alps
	Tertiary	Oligocene	37		
		Paleogene			
		Eocene	54	Whales	
		Paleocene	65	Horses, Alligators	Rockies
	Cretaceous		135		
				Birds	Sierra Nevada
Mesozoic	Jurassic		210	Mammals	Atlantic
				Dinosaurs	
	Triassic		250		
	Permian		280	Reptiles	Appalachians
	Pennsylvanian		310		Ice age
				Trees	
	Carboniferous				
Paleozoic	Mississippian		345	Amphibians	Pangaea
				Insects	
	Devonian		400	Sharks	
	Silurian		435	Land plants	Laursia
	Ordovician		500	Fish	
	Cambrian		544	Sea plants	Gondwana
				Shelled animals	
			700	Invertebrates	
Proterozoic			2500	Metazoans	
			3500	Earliest life	
Archean			4000		Oldest rocks
			4600		Meteorites

Glossary

abyssal plains—Stable, flat parts of the deep oceanic floor. They are typically covered with fine-grained sedimentary deposits called deep-sea oozes, derived from the small skeletons of siliceous organisms that fell to the seafloor.

accretion—The transfer of material, such as sedimentary rocks, from an oceanic plate to an overriding continental plate at a convergent plate margin. Less commonly the term may be applied to the addition of magma that crystallizes into rocks and is added to the extensional plate boundaries in mid-ocean ridges.

accretionary prism—A structurally complex belt of rocks formed just above a subduction zone and characterized by strongly folded and faulted rocks scraped off from the downgoing oceanic plate.

angular velocity—A measure in degrees of the change in angle per unit time as an object spins about a pivot point. If an object is rotated about a pivot point, the angular velocity stays the same with increasing distance from the pivot point, but the linear velocity (speed) will increase with distance from the pivot point.

asthenosphere—Weak partially molten layer in the Earth beneath the lithosphere, extending to about 155 miles (250 km) depth. The lithosphere slides on this weak layer, enabling plate tectonics to occur.

backarc—The part of a magmatic arc that is on the continent side of an arc, or on the side furthest from the trench. Includes backarc basins.

basalt—The most common igneous rock of the oceanic crust is called basalt, and its subvolcanic or plutonic equivalent is called gabbro. The density of basalt is 3.0 g/cm³; its mineralogy includes plagioclase, clinopyroxene, and olivine.

Benioff zone—A narrow zone of earthquakes along a convergent boundary that marks the plane of slip between a subducting plate and an overriding plate is called a Benioff zone, after its discoverer, Hugo Benioff.

body waves—Seismic waves that travel through the whole body of the Earth and move faster than surface waves. There are two types of body waves—P or compressional waves and S waves, for shear or secondary waves. P waves deform material through a change in volume and density, and these can pass through solids, liquids and gases. The kind of movement associated with passage of a P wave is a back and forth type of motion. S or secondary waves change the shape of a material, but not its volume. Only solids can transmit shear waves, whereas liquids can not. Shear waves move material at right angles to the direction of wave travel and thus they consist of an alternating series of sideways motions.

caldera—A roughly circular or elliptical depression, often occupied by a lake, that forms when the rocks above a subterranean magma mass collapse into the magma during a cataclysmic eruption.

chert—A fine-grained almost glassy siliceous chemical sedimentary rock. Many cherts are made from the siliceous tests or outer skeletons of small organisms called radiolarians. Other chert is derived from volcanic activity, and still other chert is derived by chemical precipitation from seawater.

collision zone—A zone of uplifted mountains where two continental plates or magmatic arcs have collided as a result of subduction along a convergent plate boundary.

compressional waves—See **body waves**.

convergent boundaries—Places where two plates move toward each other, resulting in one plate sliding beneath the other when a dense oceanic plate is involved, or collision and deformation, when continental plates are involved. These types of plate boundaries may have the largest of all earthquakes.

cratons—Very old and stable portions of the continents that have been inactive for billions of years, and typically have subdued topography including gentle arches and basins.

dike—Any tablular, parallel sided igneous intrusion that generally cuts across layering in the surrounding country rocks.

dilation—Expansion of a rock caused by the development of numerous minor cracks or fractures in the rocks that form in response to the stresses concentrated along the fault zone.

divergent boundaries—Divergent boundaries or margins are where two plates move apart, creating a void that is typically filled by new oceanic crust that wells up to fill the progressively opening hole.

earthquake—A sudden release of energy from slip on a fault, an explosion, or other event that causes the ground to shake and vibrate, associated with passage of waves of energy released at its source. An earthquake originates in one place and then spreads out in all directions along the fault plane.

elastic rebound theory—This theory states that recoverable (also known as elastic) strains build up in a material until a specific level or breaking point is reached. When the breaking point or level is attained, the material suddenly breaks, releasing energy and strains causing an earthquake.

epicenter—The point on the Earth's surface that lies vertically above the focus.

facies—A distinctive set of igneous, metamorphic, or sedimentary characteristics of a group of rocks that separate and differentiate them from surrounding groups of rocks.

fanglomerate—A type of sedimentary deposit in which conglomerates are deposited as an alluvial fan derived from nearby uplifted mountains.

flower structure—A distinctive geometry of faults where a major nearly vertical strike slip fault in the center of a mountain range is succeeded outward on both sides by more shallow dipping faults with strike-slip and thrust components of motion. A cross section drawn through these types of structures resembles a flower, or a palm tree.

flysch—A thick group of turbidites and shale deposited at the same time as mountain building, typically in a deep-sea basin environment or a forearc basin on a continent.

focus—The point in the Earth where the earthquake energy is first released and represents the area on one side of a fault that actually moves relative to the rocks on the other side of the fault plane. After the first slip event the area surrounding the focus experiences many smaller earthquakes as the surrounding rocks also slip past each other to even out the deformation caused by the initial earthquake shock.

forearc—The part of a magmatic arc on the oceanward side of the arc, including the forearc basin, accretionary wedge, and trench.

fracture zone—In oceanic crust, the zone that appears to be an extension of the transform fault, but is actually not a plate boundary.

Fracture zones represent the places where two parts of the same plate with different ages are juxtaposed by seafloor spreading.

geomorphology—Study of the surface features and landforms on Earth.

granite, granodiorite—Common igneous rock types in the continental crust. The density of granodiorite is 2.6 g/cm^3; its mineralogy includes quartz, plagioclase, biotite, and some potassium feldspar. Granite has more quartz than granodiorite. The volcanic or extrusive equivalent of granite is rhyolite, and of granodiorite, andesite.

granulite—A high-grade metamorphic rock formed at high pressures and temperatures, and characteristic of the middle to deep crust.

great earthquakes—Earthquakes with magnitude greater than 8.0 on the Richter scale are classified as great, for the vast amount of destruction they often cause, and the huge amount of energy released. Most great earthquakes occur at convergent plate margins.

greywacke—A sandy sedimentary rock with mud particles between the sand grains.

ground breaks—Fissures or ruptures that form where a fault cuts the surface, and may also be associated with mass wasting, or the movements of large blocks of land downhill. These ground breaks may have horizontal, vertical, or combined displacements across them and may cause considerable damage.

ground level—The elevation of the land surface above sea level.

ground motion—Shaking and other motion of the ground associated with the passage of seismic waves. The amount of ground motion associated with an earthquake generally increases with the magnitude of the earthquake, but depends also on the nature of the substratum. Ground motions are measured as accelerations, which is the rate of change of motion.

hot spot—An area of unusually active magmatic activity that is not associated with a plate boundary. Hot spots are thought to form above a plume of magma rising from deep in the mantle.

hydrothermal—Any process that involves high temperature fluids, typically used to refer to hot springs, geysers, and related activity.

intraplate earthquake—Most earthquakes occur along plate boundary zones. However, occasionally, strong earthquakes occur in the interior of plates far from plate boundaries. The origins of these earthquakes are not well understood, but are classified as intraplate earthquakes.

island arc—See **magmatic arc**.

isostasy—A principle that states that the elevation of any large segment of crust is directly proportional to the thickness of the crust.

kinematics—Study of motions without consideration of forces or stresses involved. Most of plate tectonics and structural geology are kinematic models.

liquefaction—A process where sudden shaking of certain types of water-saturated sands and muds turns these once-solid sediments into a slurry, a substance with a liquid-like consistency. Liquefaction occurs when individual grains move apart, and then water moves up in between the individual grains making the whole water/sediment mixture behave like a fluid.

lithosphere—Rigid outer shell of the Earth that is about 75 miles (125 km) thick under continents, and 45 miles (75 km) thick under oceans. The basic theorem of plate tectonics is that the lithosphere of the Earth is broken into about twelve large rigid blocks or plates that are all moving relative to one another.

mafic—Generally dark-colored igneous rocks that are composed chiefly of iron-magnesium rich minerals, and generally having silica contents between 45–52 percent as determined by chemical analysis. Common mafic igneous rocks include basalt and gabbro.

magma—Molten rock, at high temperature, is called magma. When magma flows on the surface it is known as lava.

magmatic arc—A line of volcanoes and igneous intrusions that forms above a subducting oceanic plate along a convergent margin. Island arcs are built on oceanic crust, and continental margin magmatic arcs are built on continental crust.

mass wasting—The movement of material downhill without the direct involvement of water.

mélange—A complexly mixed assemblage of rocks, characteristically formed at subduction zones.

Mercalli intensity scale—The Mercalli scale measures the amount of vibration people remember feeling for low-magnitude earthquakes, and measures the amount of damage to buildings in high-magnitude events.

metamorphism—Changes in the texture and mineralogy of a rock due to changes in the pressure, temperature, and composition of fluids, typically from plate margin processes.

mid-ocean ridge system—A 40,000-mile (65,000-km) long mountain ridge that runs through all the major oceans on the planet. The mid-ocean ridge system includes vast outpourings of young lava on the ocean floor, and represents places where new oceanic crust is being generated by plate tectonics.

Mohorovicic discontinuity—The transition from crust to mantle is generally marked by a dramatic increase in the velocity of compressional seismic waves, from typical values of less than 4.7 miles per second to values greater than 4.85 miles per second (7.6–7.8 km/sec). This boundary was first noted by the Yugoslavian seismologist Andrija Mohorovičić in his study of a Balkan earthquake in 1909. Although the Mohorovicic discontinuity is present in most places in continents at depths of several tens of kilometers, there are some regions beneath continents where there is not a significant variation between the seismic velocities of the lower continental crust and the upper mantle. In these regions the Moho (as it is familarly called) is either absent or difficult to detect. The Moho generally lies at depths of three to six miles (5–10 km) beneath most regions in the oceans. The Moho probably represents the change from basaltic or gabbroic material above to peridotitic or dunitic material below.

olistostromes—Chaotic sedimentary deposits consisting of blocks of one rock type mixed with another, and complexly folded, are called olistostromes. Most olistostromes are thought to be formed by the downslope movement of sedimentary packages.

ophiolite—A group of mafic and ultramafic rocks including pillow lavas, and plutonic and mantle rocks, generally interpreted to represent pieces of oceanic crust and lithosphere.

orogenic belts—Linear chains of mountains, largely on the continents, that contain highly deformed, contorted rocks that represent places where lithospheric plates have collided or slid past one another.

paleoseismicity—The study of past earthquakes. Most paleoseismicity studies rely on techniques such as digging trenches across faults to determine the recurrence intervals of fault segments. Some paleoseismicity studies combine archaeology with geology and look for ruins of ancient civilizations that show signs of earthquake damage, and then use isotopic or historical dating methods to determine the time of the ancient destructive earthquake.

passive continental margin—A boundary between continental and oceanic crust that is not a plate boundary, characterized by thick deposits of sedimentary rocks. These margins typically have a flat, shallow water shelf, then a steep drop off to deep ocean floor rocks away from the continent.

peridotite—A common rock of the mantle of the Earth. The average upper mantle composition is equivalent to peridotite. The density of peridotite is 3.3 g/cm^3; its mineralogy includes olivine, clinopyroxene, and orthopyroxene.

pillow lava—A form of lava flow with bulb- or pillow-like shapes, generally basaltic in composition, that forms beneath water and is common on the ocean floor.

plane strain—A type of strain or deformation of rock in which the rock is shortened in one direction, elongated in a perpendicular direction, and has no change in the third perpendicular direction.

plate tectonics—A model that describes the process related to the slow motions of more than a dozen rigid plates of solid rock around on the surface of the Earth. The plates ride on a deeper layer of partially molten material that is found at depths starting at 60–200 miles (100–320 km) beneath the surface of the continents, and 1–100 miles (1–160 km) beneath the oceans.

Plinian—A type of volcanic eruption characterized by a large and tall eruption column, typically reaching tens of thousands of feet (thousands of m) into the air. Named after Pliny the Elder, from his description of Vesuvius.

pole of rotation—When a plate moves on the globe, its motion can be uniquely described by a rotation about a pole that goes through the center of the Earth, and exits at two places on the globe, known as poles of rotation.

radiaolarian—Small microfossils from the tests (hard covering or shell) of planktonic organisms that live in the open ocean.

recurrence interval—The average repeat time for earthquakes along a specific segment of a fault, based on the statistics of how frequently earthquakes of specific magnitude occur along individual segments of faults.

Richter scale—An open-ended scale that gives an idea of the amount of energy released during an earthquake, and is based on the amplitudes (half the height from wave-base to wave-crest) of seismic waves at a distance of 62 miles (100 km) from the epicenter. The Richter scale is logarithmic, where each step of one corresponds to a tenfold increase in amplitude. Because larger earthquakes produce more waves, it turns out that an increase of one on the Richter scale corresponds to a 30 times increase in energy released. Named after Frank Richter, an American seismologist.

rifts—Elongated topographic depressions, typically with faults along their margins, where the entire thickness of the lithosphere has ruptured in extension. These are places where the continents are beginning to break apart, and if successful, may form new ocean basins.

seafloor spreading—The process of producing new oceanic crust, as volcanic basalt pours out of the depths of the Earth, filling the gaps generated by diverging plates. Beneath the mid-oceanic ridges, magma rises from a depth in the mantle and forms chambers filled with magma just below the crest of the ridges. The magma in these chambers erupts out through cracks in the roof of the chambers, and forms extensive lava flows on the surface. As the two different plates on either side of the magma chamber move apart, these lava flows continuously fill in the gap between the diverging plates, creating new oceanic crust.

seiche waves—Waves generated by the back-and-forth motion associated with earthquakes, causing a body of water (usually lakes or bays) to rock back and forth, gaining amplitude and splashing up to higher levels than normally associated with that body of water.

seismic gaps—Places along large fault zones that have little or no seismic activity compared to adjacent parts of the same fault. Seismic gaps are generally interpreted as places where the fault zone is stuck, and where adjacent parts of the fault are gradually slipping along, slowly releasing seismic energy and strains associated with the relative creeping motion of opposing sides of the fault. Since the areas of the seismic gaps are not slipping, the energy gradually builds up in these sections, until it is released in a relatively large earthquake.

seismograph—A device built to measure the amount and direction of shaking associated with earthquakes.

shear waves—See **body waves**.

slump—A type of mass wasting where a large mass of rock or sediment moves downward and outward along an upward curving fault surface. Slumps may occur undersea or on the land surface.

subduction—The destruction of oceanic crust and lithosphere by sinking back into the mantle at the deep ocean trenches. As the oceanic slabs go down, they experience higher temperatures that cause rock-melts or magma to be generated, which then move upwards to intrude the overlying plate. Since subduction zones are long, narrow zones where large plates are being subducted into the mantle, the melting produces a long line of volcanoes above the down-going plate and forms a volcanic arc. Depending on what the overriding plate is made of, this arc may be built on either a continental or an oceanic plate.

subsidence—Sinking of one surface, such as the land, relative to another surface, such as sea level.

surface waves—Waves that travel along the surface, producing complicated types of twisting and circular motions, much like the circular motions exhibited by waves out past the surf zone at the beach. Surface waves travel slower than either type of body waves, but because of their complicated types of motion they often cause the most damage.

tephra—A general term for all ash and rock fragments strewn from a volcano.

terrane—A fault-bounded block of rock that has a geologic history different from that of neighboring rocks, and likely was transported from far away by plate tectonic processes.

thrust—A contractional fault, or a reverse fault generally with shallow dips.

tidal gauge—A sensitive pressure meter placed on the sea floor that can accurately measure changes in the height of the sea surface, and used for the detection of tides, storm surges, and tsunamis.

transform boundaries—Places where two plates slide past each other, such as along the San Andreas Fault in California, and often have large earthquakes.

triple junction—Places where three plate boundaries meet.

tsunami—A giant harbor, or deepwater, wave, with long wavelengths, initiated by submarine landslides, earthquakes, volcanic eruptions, or other causes that suddenly displaces large amounts of water. Tsunamis can be much larger than normal waves when they strike the shore, and cause great damage and destruction.

turbidite—A sedimentary unit characterized by being deposited by a turbidity current. Most turbidites show a sequence of coarse-grained sands at their base, and fine silts or mud on their tops, indicting deposition during slowing of the current.

ultramafic—Dark-colored igneous rocks composed of iron-magnesium minerals, with silica contents of less than 45 percent as determined by chemical analysis. Some ultramafic igneous rocks include peridotite and komatiite.

Further Reading and Web Sites

BOOKS

Abbott, Patrick L. *Natural Disasters.* 3rd ed. Boston: McGraw Hill, 2002. This is a general college level textbook on natural disasters, intended for non-science majors.

Bolt, Bruce A. *Earthquakes,* 4th ed. New York: W. H. Freeman, 1999. This is an introductory level textbook about earthquakes and their effects.

Bryant, Edward A. *Natural Hazards.* Rev. ed. Cambridge: Cambridge University Press, 2005. This updated edition presents a comprehensive, interdisciplinary analysis of the complete range of natural hazards.

California Division of Mines and Geology. *The Loma Prieta (Santa Cruz Mountains) Earthquake of October 17, 1989.* Special Publication 104, 1990. The 1989 Loma Prieta earthquake and its effects in California are described in detail in this volume.

Coburn, A., and R. Spence, *Earthquake Protection.* Chichester, Eng.: John Wiley, 1992. This book is used by insurance and other professionals to describe how to protect life and property in earthquake prone areas.

Eldredge, N. *Life in the Balance.* Princeton, N.J.: Princeton University Press, 1998. This book discusses environmental science in the context of changing population and global change.

Erickson, Jon. *Quakes, Eruptions, and Other Geologic Cataclysms: Revealing the Earth's Hazards.* New York: Facts On File, 2001. This is a high-school level text that discusses earthquakes, volcanic eruptions, meteorite impacts, and other geologic catastrophes.

Griggs, G. B., and J. A. Gilchrist. *Geologic Hazards, Resources, and Environmental Planning.* Belmont, Calif.: Wadsworth Publishing Co., 1983. This is an advanced college-level text that integrates geology, environmental science, and community planning to reduce hazards to human populations.

Hwang, H. H. Y., ed. "Taiwan Chi-Chi Earthquake 9.21.1999, Bird's Eye View of Cher-Lung-Pu Fault." Taipei, Taiwan: Sino-Geotechnics Research and Development Foundation, 1999. Provides a detailed account of the 1999 Taiwan earthquake and its devastation across Taiwan, using many aerial photographs to illustrate the damage.

Keller, Edward A. *Environmental Geology.* 8th ed. Englewood Cliffs, N.J.: Prentice Hall, 2000. A college-level textbook meant for geological science majors entering the environmental field.

Kendrick, T. D. *The Lisbon Earthquake.* London: Methuen, 1956. Presents a detailed account of the 1775 Lisbon earthquake and tsunami.

Kusky, Timothy M. *Geological Hazards, A Sourcebook,* Westport, Conn.: Greenwood Press, 2003. This book was written for audiences at all levels from high school to professional, and includes discussion and sources for geologic hazards including earthquakes.

Logorio, H. *Earthquakes: An Architect's Guide to Non-Structural Seismic Hazards.* New York: John Wiley, 1991. This book is used by professionals to understand how to reduce earthquake hazards inside buildings.

Mackenzie, F. T., and J. A. Mackenzie. *Our Changing Planet, An Introduction to Earth System Science and Global Environmental Change.* Englewood Cliffs, N.J.: Prentice Hall, 1995. This is a general introductory level textbook for non-science majors in college, covering climate change, and issues including earthquake risks facing society.

Murck, B. W., Brian J. Skinner, and S. C. Porter. *Dangerous Earth: An Introduction to Geologic Hazards.* New York: John Wiley, 1997. This is a general introductory level textbook on earthquakes and other geologic hazards intended for the non-science major in college.

Reiter, L. *Earthquake Hazard Analysis.* New York: Columbia University Press, 1990. Insurance and real estate professionals use this book to determine the risk from earthquakes in specific regions.

Richter, C. F. *Elementary Seismology.* San Francisco: W. H. Freeman, 1958. This is an elementary textbook describing the propagation of seismic waves through the Earth.

Skinner, Brian J., and B. J. Porter. *The Dynamic Earth, an Introduction to Physical Geology.* New York: John Wiley, 1989. This is a popular, well-written textbook for introductory college classes in geology.

U.S. Geological Survey. *The Alaska Earthquake, March 27, 1964.* Geological Survey Professional Papers 542-B: *Effects on Communities–Whittier*; 542-D: *Effects on Communities–Homer*; 542-E: *Effects on Communities–Seward*; 542-G: *Effects on Communities–Various Communities*; 543-A: *Regional Effects: Slide-induced waves, seiching and ground fracturing at Kenai Lake*; 543-1: *Regional Effects–Tectonics*; 543-B: *Regional Effects–Martin-Bering Rivers area*; 543-F: *Regional Effects–Ground Breakage in the Cook Inlet area*; 543-H: *Regional Effects–Erosion and Deposition on a Raised Beach, Montague Island*; 543-J: *Regional Effects: Shore Processes and Beach Morphology*; 544-C: *Effects on Hydrologic*

Regime–Outside Alaska; 544-D: *Effects on Hydrologic Regime–Glaciers*; 544-E: *Effects on Hydrologic Regime–Seismic Seiches*; 545-A: *Effects on Transportation and Utilities–Eklutna Power Project*. Menlo Park Calif.: U.S. Geological Survey, 1966. This series of books by the U.S. Geological Survey presents descriptions of the effects of the 1964 Alaska earthquake on different communities and systems across Alaska.

U.S. Geological Survey. *Lesson learned from the Loma Prieta Earthquake of October 17, 1989*. U.S. Geological Survey, Circular 1045. Menlo Park, Calif.: 1989. In this report, the U.S. Geological Survey presents a description of the damage from the Loma Prieta earthquake, and suggests what can be done to reduce earthquake damage in the future based on the patterns of that damage.

——. *The San Francisco Earthquake and Fire of April 18, 1906*. U.S. Geological Survey Bulletin 324, 170 pages [Rare book]. Menlo Park, Calif.: U.S. Geological Survey, 1907. A thorough description of the damage resulting from the earthquake and fire of 1906, including many black and white photographs and firsthand descriptions.

Verney, Peter. *The Earthquake Handbook*. New York: Paddington Press, 1979. This book presents the reader with a basic description of earthquake hazards, and what should be done to prepare for cataclysm for those who live in earthquake zones.

Wallace, R. E. ed. *The San Andreas Fault System, California*. U.S. Geological Survey Professional Paper 1515, 1990. This is a well-illustrated book that presents many maps and descriptions of different segments of the San Andreas Fault system, and the earthquake history along each segment.

JOURNAL ARTICLES AND PERIODICALS

Boraiko, A. A. "Earthquake in Mexico." *National Geographic* 169 (1986): 654–675. There are many pictures and a general discussion of the earthquake hazards in one of the world's largest cities, Mexico City.

Earthquakes and Volcanoes. A bi-monthly publication of the U.S. Geological Survey aimed at providing current information on earthquakes and seismology, volcanoes, and related natural hazards of interest to both generalized and specialized readers. Available from "Earthquakes and Volcanoes," U.S. Geological Survey, Denver, Colo.

Kusky, Timothy M., and Farouk El-Baz. "Neotectonics and Fluvial Geomorphology of the Northern Sinai Peninsula." *Journal of African Earth Sciences* 31 (2000). This paper discusses the evidence for recent earthquake activity across the Middle East from Egypt through Israel and Lebanon to Syria.

Kusky, Timothy M., Mohamed A. Yahia, Talaat Ramadan, and Farouk El-Baz. "Notes on the Structural and Neotectonic Evolution of El-Faiyum Depression, Egypt: Relationships to Earthquake Hazards." Cairo,

Egypt: *Egyptian Journal of Remote Sensing and Space Sciences* 2 (2001). This paper discusses recent earthquakes and the seismic risk in the densely populated area of Cairo, Egypt, and the surrounding regions of North Africa.

Reilinger, Robert, N. Toksoz, S. McClusky, and A. Barka. "Izmit, Turkey earthquake was no surprise," *GSA Today* 10 (2000). This is a technical discussion of how the Izmit, Turkey, earthquake of 1999 could have been predicted.

WEB SITES

In the past few years numerous Internet Web sites that have information about earthquakes have appeared. Most of these Web sites are free, and include historical information about specific earthquakes, real-time monitoring of earthquakes around the world, and educational material. The sites listed below have interesting information and graphics about different earthquakes. This book may serve as a useful companion while surfing through the information on the Internet and encountering unfamiliar phrases, terms, or concepts that are not fully explained on the Web site. The following list of Web sites is recommended to help enrich the content of this book and make your exploration of earthquakes and earthquake hazards more enjoyable. In addition, any earthquakes that occur after this book goes to press will be discussed on these Web sites, so checking the Web sites listed here can help you keep this book up to date. From these Web sites you will also be able to link to a large variety of earthquake-related sites. Every effort has been made to ensure the accuracy of the information provided for these Web sites. However, due to the dynamic nature of the Internet, change might occur, and any inconvenience is regretted.

American Geological Institute Government Affairs Program. The AGI Government Affairs Program (GAP), established in 1992, serves as an important link between the federal government and the geoscience community. Through Congressional workshops, testimony, letters, and meetings, GAP ensures that the voices of the AGI Member Societies are heard on Capitol Hill and in the executive branch. At the same time, GAP is working to improve the flow of geoscience information to policy-makers. Equally important is the program's mission of providing federal science policy information back to the member societies and the geoscience community at large. URL: http://www.agiweb.org/gap/index.html. Accessed on August 26, 2006.

Boston College, Weston Geophysical Observatory. Department of Geology and Geophysics, 381 Concord Road, Weston, Massachusetts 02493–1340. Weston Observatory is a geophysical research laboratory of the Department of Geology and Geophysics at Boston College. The Observatory is located in the town of Weston, Massachusetts, about 13 miles west of downtown Boston. The Observatory houses seismic instruments for the World-Wide Standardized Seismic Network (WWSSN) and for the New England Seismic Network (NESN). The Observatory's staff monitors the Northeast United States for seismic activity and disseminates information pertinent to any events that are recorded. URL: http://www.bc.edu/research/westonobservatory/. Accessed on August 26, 2006.

California Institute of Technology. Seismological Laboratories, 1200 East California Boulevard, Pasadena, California 91125. Caltech's Seismological Laboratory, established in 1921, has a distinguished history of contributing to science and serving the public interest. Being internationally recognized for excellence in geophysical research and academics makes this an ideal place for study. The lab also serves as a focal point for earthquake information in southern California and the world. URL: http://www.gps.caltech.edu/seismo/. Accessed on August 26, 2006.

Edinburgh Earth Observatory. Maps of global distribution of earthquakes. This site provides up-to-date dynamic maps of earthquakes around the world, as well as a database of past earthquakes. URL: http://www.geo.ed.ac.uk/scratch/quake_all.html, Accessed August 26, 2006

Federal Emergency Management Agency. FEMA is the nation's premier agency that deals with emergency management and preparation, and issues warnings and evacuation orders when disasters appear imminent. FEMA maintains a Web site that is updated at least daily, includes information of hurricanes, floods, fires, national flood insurance, and information on disaster prevention, preparation, and emergency management. Divided into national and regional sites. Also contains information on costs of disasters, maps, and directions on how to do business with FEMA. FEMA 500 C Street, SW, Washington, D.C. 20472. URL: http://www.fema.gov. Accessed August 26, 2006.

IRIS Consortium (Incorporated Research Institutions for Seismology). The Incorporated Research Institutions for Seismology is a university research consortium dedicated to exploring the Earth's interior through the collection and distribution of seismographic data. IRIS programs contribute to scholarly research, education, earthquake hazard mitigation, and the verification of a Comprehensive Test Ban Treaty. Support for IRIS comes from the National Science Foundation, other federal agencies, universities, and private foundations. URL: http://www.iris.washington.edu. Accessed August 26, 2006.

NASA's Web Site on Natural Hazards. Earth scientists around the world use NASA satellite imagery to better understand the causes and effects of natural hazards. This site posts many public domain images to help people visualize where and when natural hazards occur, and to help mitigate their effects. All images in this section are freely available to the public for reuse or republication. URL: http://earthobservatory. nasa.gov/NaturalHazards/. Accessed August 26, 2006.

National Earthquake Information Center. The mission of the National Earthquake Information Center (NEIC) is to determine rapidly the location and size of all destructive earthquakes worldwide and to immediately disseminate this information to concerned national and international agencies, scientists, and the general public. The NEIC/WDC for Seismology compiles and maintains an extensive, global seismic database on earthquake parameters and their effects that serves as a solid foundation for basic and applied earth science research. URL: http://www.neic.cr.usgs.gov/. Accessed August 27, 2006.

Natural Hazards Observer. This Web site is the online version of the periodical, *The Natural Hazards Observer. The Natural Hazards Observer* is the bimonthly periodical of the Natural Hazards Center. It covers current disaster issues; new international, national, and local disaster management, mitigation, and education programs; hazards research; political and policy developments; new information sources and Web sites; upcoming conferences; and recent publications. Distributed to over 15,000 subscribers in the United States and abroad via printed copies from their Web site, the *Observer* focuses on news regarding human adaptation and response to natural hazards and other catastrophic events and provides a forum for concerned individuals to express opinions and generate new ideas through invited personal articles. URL: http://www.colorado.edu/hazards/o/. Accessed August 26, 2006.

San Francisco Bay Area Earthquake Hazard Information. ABAG, the Association of Bay Area Governments, is the regional planning and services agency for the nine-county San Francisco Bay Area. They maintain a Web site with information about making your home safer from earthquakes, shake potential maps, information about current and past earthquakes, and a puzzle page for kids. URL: http://quake. abag.ca.gov/. Accessed August 26, 2006.

St. Louis University Center for Environmental Science. This site has discussions of many types of geologic hazards, including earthquakes, volcanoes, tsunamis, hurricanes, and how these geologic phenomena are affecting people. URL: http//www.ces.slu.edu./ Accessed May 9, 2007.

St. Louis University Earthquake Center. The site contains information about current and historical earthquakes in the central Unites States, including the New Madrid seismic zone. Saint Louis University, Department of Earth and Atmospheric Sciences, Earthquake Center, Room 329, Macelwane Hall, 3507 Laclede Ave., Saint Louis, Missouri 63103.URL: http://www.eas.slu.edu/Earthquake_Center/Earthquakecenter.html. Accessed August 27, 2006.

University of Utah, University of Utah Seismograph Stations. 135 South 1460 East, Room 705 WBB, Salt Lake City, Utah 84112. Shows maps of recent seismicity in the intermountain west and the Yellowstone Region. URL: http://www.seis.utah.edu/recenteqs/. Accessed August 27, 2006.

U.S. Geological Survey, U.S. Department of the Interior. 345 Middle-field Road, Menlo Park, California 94025, also, offices in Reston, Va., Denver, Colo., Main Offices URL: http://www.usgs.gov/. Earthquake Hazards Program, monitors recent earthquakes world wide. The USGS is responsible for making maps of the many of the different types of earthquake hazards discussed in this book, including earthquake related shaking hazards, tsunamis, landslides, and others. This site also provides answers to frequently asked questions about earthquakes. URL: http://earthquake.usgs.gov/. Accessed August 27, 2006. U.S. Geological Survey, National Earthquake Information Center, Federal Center, Box 25046, MS 967, Denver, Colorado 80225–0046.

USGS Educational Web site for Natural Hazards. In the United States each year, natural hazards cause hundreds of deaths and cost tens of billions of dollars in disaster aid, disruption of commerce, and destruction of homes and critical infrastructure. This series of sections on this site will educate citizens, emergency managers, and lawmakers on seven natural hazards facing the nation—earthquakes, floods, hurricanes, landslides, tsunamis, volcanoes, and wildfires—and show how USGS science helps mitigate disasters and build resilient communities. URL: http://www.usgs.gov/themes/hazard.html. Accessed August 27, 2006.

Index

Note: Page numbers in *italic* refer to illustrations, *m* indicates a map, *t* indicates a table.